AND IF THIS GOSPEL

Daniel L. McNab

TEACH Services, Inc.
P U B L I S H I N G
www.TEACHServices.com • (800) 367-1844

World rights reserved. This book or any portion thereof may not be copied or reproduced in any form or manner whatever, except as provided by law, without the written permission of the publisher, except by a reviewer who may quote brief passages in a review.

The author assumes full responsibility for the accuracy of all facts and quotations as cited in this book. The opinions expressed in this book are the author's personal views and interpretations, and do not necessarily reflect those of the publisher.

This book is provided with the understanding that the publisher is not engaged in giving spiritual, legal, medical, or other professional advice. If authoritative advice is needed, the reader should seek the counsel of a competent professional.

Copyright © 2019 Daniel L. McNab
Copyright © 2019 TEACH Services, Inc.
ISBN-13: 978-1-4796-1035-8 (Paperback)
ISBN-13: 978-1-4796-1176-8 (Hardback)
ISBN-13: 978-1-4796-1036-5 (ePub)
Library of Congress Control Number: 2019907702

Unless otherwise noted, all scriptures are taken from the New King James Version®. Copyright © 1982 by Thomas Nelson. Used by permission. All rights reserved.

Scripture verses labeled (KJV) are taken from the King James Version of the Bible. Public domain.

Scripture verses labeled (ASV) are taken from the American Standard Version. Public domain.

Published by

TEACH Services, Inc.
P U B L I S H I N G
www.TEACHServices.com • (800) 367-1844

Table of Contents

Chapter 1 Jesus, What a Wonderful Savior 5

Chapter 2 The Power of Prayer. 17

Chapter 3 The Miracle of God's Grace 29

Chapter 4 Jesus, His Fulfillment of Prophecy 35

Chapter 5 Strength Through Suffering. 51

Chapter 6 Jesus Paid Our Sin-Debt with His Blood. 60

Chapter 7 Signs of Our Times 70

Chapter 8 The Wonderful Condescension of Christ 73

Chapter 9 Jesus Will Come Again 80

Chapter 10 Last Day Events 87

Chapter 11 The Certainty of Christ's Return 96

Chapter 12 God's Final Message to Planet Earth 101

Chapter 13 Do Not Neglect Salvation. 114

Chapter 14 The Holy and the Profane. 118

Chapter 15 Why Esau Lost His Birthright 124

Chapter 16 And If this Gospel Is Preached 130

Chapter 17 Jesus, the "I Am" God with Us 137

Chapter 18 Jesus, the Heart of the Gospel 146

Chapter 19 What Will Heaven Be Like? 156

Bibliography 163

CHAPTER 1

Jesus, What a Wonderful Savior

There are religious skeptics who seek to refute the Word of God in their desire to malign the virgin birth. For that reason alone, I shall endeavor to proceed slowly and carefully in this chapter to make it possible for any readers to be able to clearly understand what God has accomplished for the salvation of all who desire to be saved. To this end, it is clear that He has intentionally made the impossible possible, showing forth His marvelous and wonderful love.

Each of the four gospels has made its contribution to the story of redemption. Matthew's gospel, mainly directed to Jewish readers, declares that Jesus Christ was the long-expected Messiah and indeed the Son of God, and He fulfilled the requirements of being the promised King who would descend from David and Abraham. Matthew presented the genealogy and early recognition that Jesus proved that He was the King of the Jews. He showed evidence that Jesus fulfilled the requirements of being the promised Messiah of the Old Testament. He also presented, in an orderly manner, the threefold genealogies that confirm the legal claim that Jesus is the Son of David, as well as the Son of Abraham, through Mary.

Seven hundred years before Jesus was born, Isaiah prophesied His birth. The line of Abraham places Him in the nation of Israel, and the line of David places Him on the throne. Customarily, women did not appear in Hebrew genealogies. In a marriage, the name that the couple takes is the name of the man, not the woman. Her line ends, but the husband's line continues; it is similar today. However, in the genealogy of Jesus, we find four women. Two of them were Canaanites, one was a Moabite, and the fourth was a Hittite—all Gentiles. It was God's plan.

1. Tamar—her story appears in Genesis 38, one of the worst chapters in the Bible. Tamar is included in the genealogy because she is a sinner.
2. Rahab—her story, which is not pretty either appears in Joshua 2. After the fall of Jericho, her life was changed. She came to a knowledge of the true God. "By faith the harlot Rahab perished not with them that believed not, when she had received the spies with peace" (Heb. 11:31, KJV). She was listed in the genealogy of Jesus because she exercised faith in the living God. She came as a sinner and reached out the hand of faith; He did the rest.
3. Ruth is mentioned in Matthew 1:5. There was a law that shut her out because it is said that a Moabite or Ammonite should not enter into the congregation of the Lord (see Deut. 23:3). Although the law prohibited Ruth, there was a man, Boaz, who came into his field one day and saw her gleaning. He fell in love with her, covered her with his mantle, and brought her into the congregation of Israel. Note the grace of God available to all. We come to Him as sinners, holding out the hand of faith, and He, by His marvelous grace, saves us.
4. Bathsheba is not mentioned by name in Matthew. She is mentioned as "her *that had been the wife* of Uriah" (1:6, KJV). Her name is not mentioned because it was David's sin, not hers. God never throws overboard one of His children who sins. A sheep may get out of the fold and become lost, but Jesus the Good Shepherd always brings the lost sheep back into the fold.

Jeconiah is in this line, but his name is omitted. Joseph is also in this line, but he is not the biological father of Jesus. He gave Jesus the natural title to the throne of David because he was Mary's husband. When we look at Luke's genealogy, we find that Mary's line comes from David through his son Nathan. Joseph's line comes through the royal line through Solomon. Both Joseph and Mary had to go to Bethlehem to be enrolled for taxation because they were both from the line of David. The genealogy concludes with these lines: "And Jacob begat Joseph the husband of Mary, of whom was born Jesus, who is called Christ" (1:16, KJV).

Matthew makes it clear that Joseph was not the father of Jesus. Although he was Mary's husband, he was not Jesus' father. Luke, another gospel writer, was a Greek physician. In his account, he explains the obstetrics, clearly showing that Jesus was virgin born. Joseph was not the father of Jesus, but Mary was not unfaithful to Joseph. Jesus was not an illegitimate child. Jeremiah's prophecy reads, "A woman shall compass a man" (31:22, KJV). Jesus is the only One for whom we have any historical record of a virgin birth. If anyone wants to take the position that He was not virgin born, present your evidence.

"So all the generations from Abraham to David *are* fourteen generations; and from David until the carrying away into Babylon *are* fourteen generations; and from the carrying away into Babylon unto Christ are fourteen generations" (Matt. 1:17, KJV). To give an overall view of Old Testament perspective, Matthew put the genealogy into groups. He seems to have omitted some names in order to fit fourteen into each period.

> *Joseph was not the father of Jesus, but Mary was not unfaithful to Joseph. Jesus was not an illegitimate child.*

Matthew has shown that Joseph was not the father of Jesus. As we just saw, God gave Jeremiah the prediction of a virgin birth. It was not describing a natural birth, but a supernatural birth, which only God was able to accomplish. "Now the birth of Jesus Christ was on this wise: When as his mother Mary was espoused to Joseph, before they had come together, she was found with child of the Holy Ghost. Then Joseph her husband, being a just *man*, and not willing to make her a publick example, was minded to put her away privily" (vs. 18, 19, KJV).

The Mosaic Law was very emphatic on this point. It said that a woman who was guilty of being unfaithful should be stoned to death. That was an extreme penalty. However, Joseph was a remarkable man. We devote a great deal of attention to Mary, and rightly so. She was a remarkable woman. Remember that she was the one whom God chose to be the mother of our Lord, and He makes no mistakes. He selected the right person.

We must also remember that God also chose Joseph, and He made no mistake in choosing him either. A hotheaded man would have immediately had her stoned to death or exposed to make her a public example. Joseph was not that kind of person. He was of a gentle disposition. He was in love with Mary and did not want to hurt her in any way, although he felt that she had been unfaithful to him. However, while he thought about these things, the angel appeared to him in a dream and said, "Joseph, thou son of David, fear not to take unto thee Mary thy wife: for that which is conceived in her is of the Holy Ghost. And she shall bring forth a son, and thou shalt call his name JESUS: for he shall save his people from their sins." (vs. 20, 21, KJV).

To prevent a very tragic situation, the angel appeared to Joseph to make clear to him what was taking place. "Now all this was done, that it might be fulfilled which was spoken of the Lord by the prophet," then Matthew recalls the prophecy of Isaiah 7:14: "Behold, a virgin shall be with child, and shall bring forth a son, and they shall call his name Emmanuel, which being interpreted is, God with us" (vs. 22, 23, KJV).

> For unto us a Child is born, Unto us a Son is given; And the government will be upon His shoulder. And His name will be called Wonderful, Counselor, Mighty God, Everlasting Father, Prince of Peace. Of the increase of *His* government and peace *There will be* no end, Upon the throne of David and over His kingdom, To order it and establish it with judgement and justice From that time forward, even forever. The zeal of the LORD of hosts will perform this. (Isaiah 9:6, 7)

The prophet Micah also predicted, "But you, Bethlehem Ephrathah, *Though* you are little among the thousands of Judah, *Yet* out of you shall come forth to Me The One to be ruler in Israel, Whose goings forth *are* from of old, From everlasting" (5:2). Matthew 1:23 enlarges the prophecy of Isaiah 7:14, as we just saw. The name "Emmanuel" was first used by Isaiah and interpreted to mean that God was with His people, the Jewish nation. The Messiah's name is Jesus. Why? Because it means "savior." "Christ" is His title (the Greek equivalent of "Messiah").

Let us look at one area of controversy that is of vital importance among some Bible commentators. They claim that the virgin birth is false. Refer back to Isaiah 7:14 and Matthew 1:23. Mary's son was named Jesus, rather than Emmanuel. This emphasizes that He would save His people from their sins. With that said, He cannot be the Savior unless He is God; He cannot be God with us unless He is virgin born.

The reason He is called Jesus is that He is God with us. Regarding this truth about the Savior, Paul says:

> For [God] has not put the world to come, of which we speak, in subjection to angels. But one testified in a certain place, saying: "What is man that You are mindful of him, Or the son of man that You take care of him? You have made him a little lower than the angels; You have crowned Him with glory and honor, And set him over the works of Your hands. You have put all things in subjection under His feet." For in that He put all in subjection under him, He left nothing *that is* not put under him. But now we do not see all things put under him. But we see Jesus, who was made a little lower than the angels, for the suffering of death crowned with glory and honor, that He, by the grace of God, might taste death for everyone. (Hebrews 2:5–9)

Jesus had to be a sacrifice that was acceptable. I could not die for the sins of the world. I could not even die a redeeming death for my sins. But Jesus could, and He did. Jesus qualified because He is Emmanuel; God with us. How did He get with us? Because He was and is without sin. He was Virgin born! He was called Jesus. He was never called Emmanuel. However, you cannot call Him Jesus, unless He is Emmanuel, God with us (McGee 1983). He continues: "You may not have to know this to be saved. But after you have become a child of God, you will not deny the Virgin Birth of our Lord and Savior Jesus Christ."

If Jesus was just another man like me, then He could never be my Savior. However, He was virgin born. He took upon Himself our humanity in this manner so that He might taste death for us—that He might die a redemptive death on the cross for us. All of the prophecies concerning the Messiah were fulfilled in Jesus of Nazareth. Almost all who have looked into this are amazed that all the Messianic prophecies found their fulfillment in Jesus Christ, the Son of God and earthly descendant of Abraham and David.

The prophet Isaiah also spoke of John the Baptist as the one who would prepare the way for the coming of the Messiah:

> The voice of one crying in the wilderness: "Prepare the way of the LORD; Make straight in the desert A highway for our God. Every valley shall be exalted And every mountain and hill shall be made low; The crooked places shall be made straight And the rough places smooth; The glory of the LORD shall be revealed, And all flesh shall see *it* together; For the mouth of the LORD has spoken." (Isaiah 40:3, 4)

John and Jesus were cousins. John was six months older than the Messiah was, but they had not met before Jesus came to John, asking to be baptized.

> Now in the sixth month the angel Gabriel was sent by God to a city of Galilee named Nazareth, to a virgin betrothed to a man whose name was Joseph, of the house of David. The virgin's name *was* Mary. And having come in, the

angel said to her, "Rejoice, highly favored *one,* the Lord *is* with you; blessed *are* you among women!" But when she saw *him,* she was troubled at his saying, and considered what manner of greeting this was. Then the angel said to her, "Do not be afraid, Mary, for you have found favor with God. And behold, you will conceive in your womb and bring forth a Son, and shall call His name Jesus. He will be great, and will be called the Son of the Highest; and the Lord God will give Him the throne of His father David. And He will reign over the house of Jacob forever, and of His kingdom there will be no end." Then Mary said to the angel, "How can this be, since I do not know a man?" And the angel answered and said to her, "*The* Holy Spirit will come upon you, and the power of the Highest will overshadow you; therefore, also, that Holy One who is to be born will be called the Son of God. Now indeed, Elizabeth your relative has also conceived a son in her old age; and this is now the sixth month for her who was called barren. For with God nothing will be impossible." Then Mary said, "Behold the maidservant of the Lord! Let it be to me according to your word." And the angel departed from her. Now Mary arose in those days and went into the hill country with haste, to a city of Judah, and entered the house of Zacharias and greeted Elizabeth. (Luke 1:26–40)

There are four gospel writers, and each one wrote from a different point of view. They seemed to have different audiences. Matthew wrote to explain that Jesus was Israel's long-expected Messiah. His gospel was directed to a Jewish audience.

Luke was a physician, and this is clear as we notice his attention to details regarding explanations of the birth of Jesus and surrounding the crucifixion and burial scenes. Luke is the only gospel writer who was not Jewish. He wrote in a style that would be appealing to Gentiles.

Mark, perhaps writing his gospel before the other three did, was not one of the disciples of Jesus. He was mentored by Simon Peter and is believed to have obtained much of his information and details from him.

John was the fourth gospel writer. Additionally, this disciple wrote three epistles and the book of Revelation (The Apocalypse), which was given to the resurrected Christ by God the Father. Jesus sent and signified it by His angel to His servant (see Rev. 1:1). John clearly states his reason for writing his gospel: "that you may believe" (John 20:31), When he wrote his account toward the end of the first century AD, there were three major dangers that threatened his life and purity as he was severely persecuted for his faith in Jesus. He wanted to encourage Christians everywhere.

If the Father, Son, and Holy Spirit had not, in ages past, before They created the world, decided to provide a way of redeeming mankind if the race should sin, we wouldn't exist today.

There was a decline in piety. Heresies such as Gnosticism, which denied the reality of the incarnation, spawned libertinism and eventually the rise of persecution in the early church. John was severely persecuted for his faith in Jesus, yet believed that people needed a vivid picture of the Savior to strengthen their faith in the reality of the great truths of the gospel. This disciple referred to himself as the disciple whom Jesus loved. He and his ten apostolic brothers (not including Judas Iscariot) were trained by the Savior to carry on the work of building the church, which He had founded by His precious blood.

Down through the centuries, others came along and, by the power of the Holy Spirit, carried on where their predecessors had left off. Today, in these last days before the return of Jesus, we are, by the grace and mercies of God in Christ, called upon to hold firmly and move forward. Jesus is coming soon! He has commanded us to hold fast. There is no doubt that it is just wonderful what God, in Christ, has done to save humanity. If the

Father, Son, and Holy Spirit had not, in ages past, before They created the world, decided to provide a way of redeeming mankind if the race should sin, we wouldn't exist today. This plan was God's great secret, securely hidden in ages past, from before the foundations of the world were laid.

When Adam sinned, God promised to send a deliverer (see Gen. 3:15). He fulfilled His promise, but His people rejected Him. Although the evidence was right there in front of them, they asked, "How can this be?" They forgot that Jesus had to suffer and die for our sins at His first coming, but now He is coming again, and every eye will see Him. The apostle Paul said it well, essentially writing that Christ humbled Himself at His first coming to be our Savior. He suffered, died, and arose the third day.

The prophet Isaiah wrote that He was bruised for our iniquities, and with His stripes, we are healed (see 53:5). Yes, it pleased the LORD to bruise His Son, but Jesus suffered it all for our redemption and the glory of the Father. Jesus—oh, what a wonderful name! It brings music to the believers' ears. The name of Jesus is so sweet.

> Let this mind be in you which was also in Christ Jesus, who, being in the form of God, did not consider it robbery to be equal with God, but made Himself of no reputation, taking the form of a bondservant, *and* coming in the likeness of men. And being found in appearance as a man, He humbled Himself and became obedient to *the point of* death, even the death of the cross. Therefore God also has highly exalted Him and given Him the name which is above every name, that at the name of Jesus every knee should bow, of those in heaven, and of those on earth, and of those under the earth, and *that* every tongue should confess that Jesus Christ *is* Lord to the glory of God the Father. (Philippians 2:5–11)

The family tree of our Lord and Savior, therefore, had to show that He was of the earthly line of Abraham. It also had to show that He was legitimately of the royal line of David, the king of Israel. Let us, therefore, trace His family tree to see if this proves to be true. It would be impossible to convince a Jew that Jesus was the Messiah sent from God unless it could be shown that He descended from David. The prophet Jeremiah predicted, "'Behold, *the* days are coming,' says the LORD, 'That I will raise to David a Branch of righteousness; A king shall reign and prosper, And execute judgment and righteousness in the earth. In His days Judah will be saved, And Israel will dwell safely; Now this *is* His name by which He will be called: THE LORD OUR RIGHTEOUSNESS'" (23:5, 6). "For your servant David's sake, Do not turn away the face of Your Anointed. The LORD has sworn *in* truth to David; He will not turn from it: 'I will set upon your throne the fruit of your body'" (Ps. 132:10, 11).

The promise was also made to Abraham: "I will bless those who bless you, And I will curse him who curses you; And in you all the families of the earth shall be blessed" (Gen. 12:3). The Jews expected that the Messiah would descend from Abraham. It was, therefore, necessary to trace the genealogy to Abraham as well. Although Jesus was of humble birth, He descended from the most illustrious ancestors. Abraham, the father of the faithful and model of eastern princes, and King David, the sweet psalmist of Israel, conqueror, and magnificent and victorious leader of the people of God.

From these two, notable, eminent, pious, most excellent persons of antiquity, the Lord Jesus descended through His earthly lineage. Despite His humble birth, those who consider an illustrious ancestry to be valuable may herein find purity, piety, patriotism, valor, dignity, and renown. No passage of Scripture has been more difficult to explain than Matthew 1:2–16; Luke 3 also has Jesus' genealogy. Many names found in the Old Testament are omitted in both Matthew and Luke.

From Abraham to David, the two ancestries are similar. The difficulty lies in the ancestries from David to Christ. They are different. Not only are the names different, but Luke mentioned forty-two names, while Matthew mentioned only twenty-seven (including David in both cases). Various methods have been proposed to resolve this difficulty, but it must be mentioned that none of them is satisfactory. It must also be mentioned that in nothing are mistakes more likely to occur than such ancestries. Because of the similarity of names, different names by which the same person is often called, and many other reasons, errors would be more likely to creep into genealogical ancestries than into other writings.

Many interpreters have supposed that Matthew gave the genealogy of Joseph, while Luke gave that of Mary. Both Mary and Joseph descended from David, but through different lines. This solution derives some reasonableness from the fact that the promise was made to David, and since Jesus was not the son of Joseph, it was necessary to show that Mary also descended from David, yet the evidence of that was important. However, it cannot be disproved that this was not Luke's intention.

It has also been implied that Joseph was the legal son and heir of Heli, though the real son of Jacob, and therefore the two lines terminated in him. This was the explanation suggested and is the most satisfactory. It was the law of the Jews that if a man died without children, his brother should marry his widow. Thereby the two lines might have been intermingled.

According to this solution, Matthan descended from Solomon and married Estha, of whom was born Jacob. After Matthan's death, Matthat, being of the same tribe but another family, married his widow, and through this marriage, Heli was born. Jacob and Heli were, therefore, children of the same mother. Heli died without children, so his brother Jacob married his widow and begat Joseph. Luke says that Joseph was the son of Heli—that is, his legal heir—and reckoned in the law to be his son.

```
              David
               /\
        Solomon  Nathan
           |       |
    Matthan  Estha  Matthat
           \       /
      Jacob < wife of both > Heli
              \ /
             JOSEPH
```

First Division (of fourteen)	Second Division	Third Division
Abraham	David	Josias
Isaac	Solomon	Jechonias
Jacob	Roboam	Salathiel
Judas	Abia	Zorobabel
Phares	Asa	Abiud
Esrom	Josaphat	Eliakim
Aram	Joram	Azor
Ammadab	Ozias	Saloe
Naasson	Joatham	Achim
Salmon	Achaz	Eliud
Booz	Ezekias	Eliazar
Obed	Manasses	Matthan
Jesse	Amon	Jacob
David	Josias	Joseph

CHAPTER 2

The Power of Prayer

Families and churches that pray together usually stay together, for when we come to the throne of grace united, as with one mind as we worship, and petition God our Creator, we are assured that He hears us, is pleased as His children come to Him, and will answer. Nothing appeals to the heart of our heavenly Father more than when His children come to Him in prayer. That has been His plan from before the foundation of the world.

God's promise is that He will answer when we come to Him in faith in the name of His dear Son, our Lord and Savior Jesus Christ. When Jesus was here on earth, His disciples often watched Him in communion with His

Father in heaven. He was so often seen in prayer that His disciples never asked Him to teach them the art of preaching. Instead, they asked Him, "Lord, teach us to pray, as John also taught his disciples" (Luke 11:1).

Jesus, the Master Teacher, also knew how to awaken the interest of His pupils. He waited until they were ready to learn. When He had piqued their interest, and they were ready, He knew they would ask. He was teaching them how to draw people, and He knew just how to direct their attention to the imperative things of the kingdom; things that were so very important for all true kingdom seekers down through the centuries, even to these last days before His return; days when the enemy of our souls would be so very busy.

How poor and meager, therefore, is our feeble praying. The saints of God's kingdom are in need of radical praying today—even much more than our necessary food—compared to such great prayer warriors in ages past. Oh, Father, how poor and meager is our childish intercessions when compared to the magnanimous blessings You yearn to lavish upon us, your children, day after day. The air and sunlight sustain life, even as You give energy that enables our frames to maintain our being.

> *Nothing appeals to the heart of our heavenly Father more than when His children come to Him in prayer.*

These blessings that we take for granted give us ever-increasing faith. Oh, Christ of Calvary, may we believe in Your promises, for Your Word is true and promises sure. "Lord in the morning Thou shalt hear my voice ascending high; To Thee direct my prayer; To Thee will I lift up my eye" (Aaron Williams, "In the Morning"). We are living in a time of earth's history when many who profess to teach God's sacred Word do not believe the things they teach others to believe.

That is like salespeople trying to sell products in which they have no confidence. Human nature wants to receive answers to prayers without expending any effort. It is therefore little wonder that those to whom we bring the gospel story seem to find it hard to believe. Our Savior, in His instructions on prayer, said that we are to "Ask, and it will be given to you; seek, and you will find; knock, and it will be opened to you. For everyone who asks receives, and he who seeks finds, and to him who knocks [heaven's storehouse] will be opened" (Matt. 7:7, 8).

God has told us in Scripture that we have not because we ask not. He has provided prayer as a means for us to communicate with Him. We can approach Him at anytime and anywhere, day or night, to pray, confess our sins, give Him adoration and praise, thank Him for His grace, mercies, and giving His Son Jesus Christ at a great sacrifice to redeem us from our sins and the pit of hell. We make requests to God for ourselves and on behalf of others. We come to listen to Him as He speaks to us in the secret place of prayer. We know that He hears us and will answer our petitions when we pray according to His will.

Saints of old, like Moses, Hannah, David, Hezekiah, Solomon, and Daniel, as well as, more recently, George Mueller, David Livingstone, and so many others who have gone before us—saints of God and His Christ who depended on prayer to sustain them when the going became rough—have set the examples for us to follow. In every situation, believers know that our Father in heaven hears and answers when we come to Him in prayer and meditation. Our Savior has promised, "If you abide in Me, and My words abide in you, you will ask what you desire, and it shall be done for you. By this My Father is glorified, that you bear much fruit; so you will be My disciples" (John 15:7, 8).

The promises of God in Christ are sure. He will fulfill every one according to His will. Jesus taught His followers to pray, "Our Father who is in heaven, hallowed is Your name." His name is honored in two ways: 1) By divine actions that lead people to acknowledge and reverence Jehovah as God (see Ex. 15:14, 15; Josh. 2:11; Ps. 145:4, 6, 12) and 2) people according Him the worship and obedience that are His due (see Isa. 58:13; Matt. 7:21–23; Acts 10:35).

"Thy kingdom come" speaks of the reign of God's gracious acts and acknowledgment of His glory and majesty. Throughout the ages, the promise that the kingdoms of this world will eventually give way to the everlasting kingdom of God and His Christ has been delivered through His various servants. "Thy kingdom come. Thy will be done on earth, as *it is* in heaven. Give us this day our daily bread. And forgive our debts, as we forgive" all those who hurt us and love them as brothers and sisters should love one another (Matt. 6:10–12, KJV). And we know that when we pray, He hears us. Then we leave all things to the will of our heavenly Father.

Again, Scripture assures us that those who come to God believing that He lives will never be disappointed. He hears and answers when we pray. Jesus taught us that those who believe that God exists and will hear and answer when we pray would live a life marked by joy. I am aware that I have repeated this often; that is because I am praying that this fact will become riveted in your consciousness and you will never be disappointed. That means that we must come to Him in faith and full assurance that He will hear us.

Hebrews 11:6 says, "But without faith it is impossible to please *Him*, for he who comes to God must believe that He is [God our Creator; real; alive and active in the universe], and *that* He is a rewarder of those who diligently seek Him." No matter how little faith one possesses, if it is exercised, God will respond to that little faith, and if we ask, He will increase it. The problem is that many people may half-heartedly pray but do not expect an answer. He has given us numerous opportunities to come to Him in prayer. When we do, we are to anticipate an answer, for He will always respond to our prayers at the right time and in the way that is appropriate for the fulfillment of His will and glory of His name.

In Scripture, God challenges us to test Him, and He has never failed. The number of people who either say they are not sure that God will answer when they pray or have not kept pace to know if God did answer is surprising. These are those of little faith. If only they knew how much they are depriving themselves of the tremendous blessings God is waiting to bestow upon them. There are times when we have a lot to say as we pour out our burdens to the Lord and express our adoration, praise, and thankfulness. Our prayers do not need to be long.

There are examples of long and short prayers in the Bible. The prophet Daniel prayed, appealing to God on behalf of his people, the Jews, who were captives in Babylon, and for the temple in Jerusalem, which was in need of restoration (see Daniel 9). King Solomon's prayer at the time his temple was dedicated to God is recorded in 2 Chronicles 6:14–42. God's response to Solomon's prayer is recorded in 2 Chronicles 7:12–22.

There are no unanswered prayers. God will always answer "yes," "no," or "wait," depending on His plans for us, for He sees and knows what time is right for the fulfillment of His will in our lives. A certain hymn often comes to mind: "Come ev'ry soul by sin oppressed, There's mercy in the Lord, And He will surely give you rest, By trusting in his word. Only trust Him, only trust Him, Only trust Him now; He will save you, he will save you, He will save you now" (J.H. Stockton, "Only Trust Him").

Sometimes, one may imagine our heavenly Father with a twinkle in His eyes and a smile on His face when His child prays, just as any earthly father would have when responding to his children.

Sometimes, one may imagine our heavenly Father with a twinkle in His eyes and a smile on His face when His child prays, just as any earthly father would have when responding to his children.

I say this with humility and awe. There have been occasions when before I put thoughts into words, the answer came. At other times, I needed to wait. We should not treat our heavenly Father like a piggy-bank of convenience. As the Bible says, come before Him with thankful hearts and into His presence with thanksgiving.

Do you not get a great deal of satisfaction when your children show appreciation for your answers to their requests? So also does our heavenly Father when we come with thankful hearts before Him. How long can we live without breathing? Did any of us summon the sun to rise over the horizon this morning? We cannot take the next breath unless your Father in heaven wills it. He holds our very existences in the palm of His hand. He gives us the energy to go about our daily affairs. He wakes us from sleep each day. He gives us the energy and opportunity to earn a living each day.

Whether we realize it or not, we are fully dependent upon God for our daily survival. In the whole universe, God is the only immortal being, and we owe honor, adoration, worship, and praise to Him. We owe Almighty God everything, especially for His gift of salvation. He gave His only Son, Christ Jesus, who humbled Himself by taking on the form of humanity and coming to this dark planet to die, giving His lifeblood to pay the ransom for every man, woman, boy, and girl who has ever lived, that they who accept Him may enjoy the riches of everlasting life.

God loves each person far more than we will ever know. Yes, respect is due to all others, but worship, adoration, and praise belong only to God. Everything in this world belongs to Him. He owns the cattle upon a thousand hills. He has loaned it all to us. My timetable is not God's timetable, but He is always on time. All others, at the end of their allotted time, die, but only the Triune God lives on eternally.

God's well-known response to Solomon's prayer includes His promise of blessings to him and the nation:

> "[I]f My people who are called by My name will humble themselves, and pray and seek My face, and turn from their wicked ways, then I will hear from heaven, and will forgive their sin and heal their land. Now My eyes will be open and My ears attentive to prayer *made* in this place. For now I have chosen and sanctified this house, that My name may be there forever; and My eyes and My heart will be there perpetually. As for you, if you walk before Me as your father David walked, and do according to all that I have commanded you, and if you keep My statutes and My judgments, then I will establish the throne of your kingdom, as I covenanted with David your father, saying, 'You shall not fail to *have* a man as ruler in Israel.' But if

you turn away and forsake My statutes and My commandments which I have set before you, and go and serve other gods, and worship them, then I will uproot them from My land which I have given them; and this house which I have sanctified for My name I will cast out of My sight, and will make it a proverb and a byword among all peoples. (2 Chronicles 7:14–20)

God always keeps His promises. Take note that all His promises to King Solomon and the nation were fulfilled, even to the latter portion. God loves everyone. That is who He is—love. When we become children of God, He loves us more than any loving, earthly parents love their children. He corrects us when necessary to bring us back in line.

We do not cease to be sons and daughters when we get out of line, but children at times need to be corrected, and that is a sign that God's everlasting love always enfolds us. If you find yourself receiving correction, then be joyful, draw closer to your heavenly Father, and be assured that He wraps you in His love, especially as He prepares you for life with Him in His paradise above someday—when Jesus comes again.

As we are dealing with the subject of prayer to our everlasting Father, permit me to recommend that to the triune God, there is no yesterday or tomorrow. Here on earth, we live in three dimensions. God exists on a much higher level. If our first parents had not yielded to the temptation to disobey God, I can only imagine how much higher humanity would have reached. We need to trust in the wisdom of our Lord and Savior Jesus Christ.

> "Eye has not seen, nor ear heard, nor have entered into the heart of man The things which God has prepared for those who love Him." But God has revealed *them* to us through His Spirit. For the Spirit searches all things, yes, the deep things of God.... Now we have received, not the spirit of the world, but the Spirit who is from God, that we

might know the things that have been freely given to us by God. (1 Corinthians 2:9, 10, 12)

When one accepts the truth of God's Word in Christ (see John 1:1–5, 14), the Holy Spirit enters our lives, and His power begins to change our hearts, cultivate a close relationship with Him, and teach more about heavenly things. It takes faith to follow Jesus, and even that faith is the gift of God. When, at times, others may laugh, mock, or even scorn as foolishness, He gives the power to press onward as we walk the Christian walk of faith. The laughing and mocking are because they have hardened their hearts to the call of the Holy Spirit on their lives.

When we commit our lives to follow in the footsteps of Jesus each day, we realize how sweet it is to serve Him. We come to appreciate how much He has done to save us. Yes, it takes faith to serve the Lord, and it gets sweeter each succeeding day. I am not saying the walk of faith is a smooth journey, but with Jesus, as we learn to trust Him, we find that the joys of serving Him far outweigh the difficulties as we see how marvelous life becomes.

One cannot have all the answers before the journey, for then it is not faith. We are called to trust in God's promises and learn of Him day by day. He gives us prayer as the means by which we speak with Him, and we hear from Him as we read and meditate upon His Word. When we pray to our Father in heaven, we come to Him in faith, confident that He will answer our prayers. When Jesus taught His disciples to pray when He was here on this earth, He instructed them to ask, seek, and knock, meaning that if our requests are in His will, we are to persist in asking, knowing that our Father in heaven will answer our requests (see Matt. 6:5–13).

There are also other guidelines Jesus gave that are necessary to receive answers to our prayers (see vs. 14, 15; 7:1–12). It is not only to receive gifts that we come to God in prayer. We come to Him and offer prayers of adoration, worship, and praise for the Father, Son, and Holy Spirit, the only Beings to whom we should pray. If prayers are offered to any other being, that would be idolatry, which is very displeasing to God.

We do not always offer prayer to our heavenly Father in the company of others, although by doing so we encourage each other. Neither is it always necessary to vocalize our prayers. There is great satisfaction we can obtain through secretly communing with God. His Holy Spirit even takes our unspoken thoughts and presents them before the Father's throne, where today, Christ our Great High Priest intercedes for all those who trust in Him. Ever since He rose from the dead and returned to heaven, Scripture assures us that He has been interceding for us before God's throne. We do not need to have any other human intercede for us.

Christ is our advocate in the heavenly sanctuary and the only intercessor that we need. Job was led to ask, "Is not God in the height of heaven? And see the highest stars, how lofty they are! And you say, 'What does God know? Can He judge through the deep darkness? Thick clouds cover Him, so that He cannot see, and He walks above the circle of heaven' … Yet He filled their houses with good *things*" (22:12–14, 18).

David wrote, "Bless the LORD, Oh my soul! O LORD my God, You are very great" (Ps. 104:1). "Oh, give thanks to the LORD, for *He is* good! For His mercy *endures* forever!" (106:1). We need to understand that Jehovah in the Old Testament is Christ in the New Testament. He is Jehovah in the burning bush who spoke to Moses. He is the everlasting God who created heaven and earth. He is the incarnate Christ in Bethlehem's manger—the same yesterday, today, and forever.

When we pray to God, asking for blessings, He promises to respond according to His will. Although the answer may seem delayed, it is always on time. If we don't receive the response we expect, the time may not be right, or it may not be in our best interest. If we wait, we will see that our best interests are served in God's time, for He knows what is best for us. He desires to give good gifts to His children, and He has already given the best gift to humanity. All that remains is for each person to claim that best and precious gift, God's only Son, the Lord Jesus Christ.

> "Likewise the Spirit also helps in our weaknesses. For we do not know what we should pray for as we ought, but the

Spirit Himself makes intercessions for us with groanings which cannot be uttered. Now He who searches the hearts knows what the mind of the Spirit *is*, because He makes intercession for the saints according to *the will of* God. And we know that all things work together for good to those who love God, to those who are the called according to *His* purpose. For whom He foreknew, He also predestined *to be* conformed to the image of His Son, that He might be the firstborn among many brethren. Moreover whom He predestined, these He also called; whom He called, these He also justified; and whom He justified, these He also glorified. What then shall we say to these things? If God *is* for us, who *can be* against us? He who did not spare His own Son, but delivered Him up for us all, how shall He not with Him also freely give us all things? Who shall bring a charge against God's elect? *It is* God who justifies. (Romans 8:26–33)

In prayer, a delay is often a test of the strength of our faith, for faith gathers strength by waiting. Nothing can be more distinct or unlimited in application, urgency, and expedience than the exhortation of Christ. Faith gives birth to prayer and grows stronger, strikes deeper, and rises higher in the struggles and wrestling of asking, seeking, and knocking. "Now faith is the substance of things hoped for, the evidence of things not seen" (Heb. 11:1).

Faith in Christ, like nothing else, can renew health and spiritual vitality, even as it motivates us to work in God's vineyard. He will always respond to the prayer of faith and supply the right answer. It is His design to reveal Himself in His providence and grace. The object of our prayers must be the glory of God, not ourselves.

"In secret prayer the soul should be laid bare to the inspecting eye of God.... How precious is secret prayer--the soul communing with

God! Secret prayer is to be heard only by the prayer-hearing God. No curious ear is to receive the burden of petitions" (White 1964, p. 272). Especially in these last days, it is even more necessary to spend time in prayer to our heavenly Father through our Lord and Savior Jesus Christ. We ought to always pray in full confidence that He will hear and answer.

The Christian's walk of faith is not often smooth. Jesus warned His followers that troublesome times would come.

> If the world hates you, you know that it hated Me before *it hated* you. If you were of the world, the world would love its own. Yet because you are not of the world, but I chose you out of the world, therefore the world hates you. Remember the word that I said to you, "A servant is not greater than his master." If they persecuted Me, they will also persecute you. If they kept My word, they will keep yours also. (John 15:18–20; see also 1 Peter 4:12–16)

Our Savior wants to make it clear that the pathway to heaven is not always smooth. However, if you ask any sincere believer, I doubt any would exchange the journey for anything this world can offer. It is wonderful to know that God the Father, through Jesus Christ, keeps His word. Prayer clears our vision, for our view is enlarged and horizon made brighter when we abide in the wisdom and will of the Lord. We catch glimpses of His glories that are awaiting those who, by faith, follow in the footsteps of our Savior. If only we could grasp what a powerful weapon Christ's followers have in prayer.

In faith, the believer is assured of God's attention when we pray. The only reason for believers not receiving answers to their petitions is a lack of faith, for Jesus repeatedly promises us that according to our faith, the answers come when we pray. When we live according to the will of God, there is every confirmation that He, in Christ, will respond to persistent prayer in all things, in ways that you and I may not understand, but further His will.

Jesus says that we are to pray in all situations and trust Him in all things. As we pray, may our minds be on Jesus and His perfect will. May the Holy Spirit guide us, that we will "Be anxious for nothing, but in everything by prayer and supplication, with thanksgiving, let your requests be made known unto God; and the peace of God, which surpasses all understanding, will guard your hearts and minds through Christ Jesus" (Phil. 4:6, 7). Amen.

CHAPTER 3

The Miracle of God's Grace

This chapter is significantly predicated on John 6:43–59. The gospel has not been preached until the meaning of the blood of Christ has been explained. It may be offensive to people, but just think of how offensive our sins are. The cost of redemption is the very life of God's only Son. Of course, it is not pretty, but our sins are not pretty in His sight either. It is only when we understand the ugliness of our sins that we will begin to understand the price that was necessary to redeem us.

There should be no doubt that salvation is the miracle of God's marvelous grace, manifested in the self-sacrifice of His only Son, Jesus Christ. Before the incarnation of our Redeemer, He was in the bosom of the Father throughout eternity, enraptured in His love. This is the reason Jesus could say with confidence, "I and *My* Father are one" (John 10:30). He also declared, "Have I been with you so long, and yet you have not known Me, Phillip? He who has seen Me has seen the Father" (14:9).

God called Israel out of Egypt to be His chosen people through whom He would bring salvation to the entire world. During their forty years of wilderness travel, He fed them with manna (bread) sent down from heaven. This heavenly food sustained the Israelites with all the nutrients necessary to enhance life and thrive. During this long journey, there was no malnutrition or disease among the people. It was only when they disobeyed God that any sickness was found among them.

Centuries later, when Jesus Christ, God's Lamb for sinners slain, came to earth to pay the ultimate sacrifice through the miracle of the incarnation and virgin birth, they declared that Moses gave them bread from heaven to eat. He replied, "I am the living bread which came down from heaven" (6:51). Jesus came down from heaven to this earth. "And the Word was made [born] flesh, and dwelt among us" (1:14, KJV).

> Jesus therefore answered and said to them, "Do not murmur among yourselves. No one can come to Me unless the Father who sent me draws him; and I will raise him up at the last day.... Therefore everyone who has heard and learned from the Father comes to Me.... he who believes in Me has everlasting life. I am the bread of life. Your fathers ate the manna in the wilderness, and are dead.... I am the living bread which came down from heaven. If anyone eats of this bread, he will live forever; and the bread that I shall give him is My flesh, which I shall give for the life of the world." The Jews quarreled among themselves, saying, "How can this Man give us *His* flesh to eat?" Then Jesus said to them, "Most assuredly, I say to you, unless you eat the flesh of the Son of Man and drink His blood. you have no life in you. Whoever eats My flesh and drinks My blood has eternal life, and I will raise him up at the last day." (John 6:43–54)

It is not enough to have spiritually partaken of His flesh once. His followers must continually in a spiritual sense feed upon Him in order to be spiritually nourished by Him who is the "Bread of Life" who came down from heaven. He came to reveal God to mankind, and to be God's sacrifice for humanity's sins. From the statements made by Jesus, it is clear that His words quoted above and below, are to be interpreted as indicated, and be spiritually understood. It seems clear that our Lord intended that a spiritual interpretation in preparing the disciples for the Lord's Supper which Jesus intended to be a memorial of His sacrifice of Himself on the cross as payment for our sins.

The life of the flesh is in the blood (Leviticus 17:11; Gen.9:4). To eat His flesh, and drink His blood signified receiving Him personally by faith. To the Jews who heard Jesus speak, and recognized the prohibition against ingesting the blood of the sacrificial animal since the blood is the life; must have understood that to eat His flesh, and drink His blood was to appropriate His life by faith. "Because Christ gave His human life for us, meant that we may partake of His divine eternal life.

> "For My flesh is food indeed, and My blood is drink indeed. He who eats My flesh and drinks My blood abides in Me, and I in him. As the living Father sent Me, and I live because of the Father, so he who feeds on Me will live because of Me. This is the bread which came down from heaven—not as your fathers ate the manna, and are dead. He who eats this bread will live forever." These things He said in the synagogue as He taught in Capernaum. (John 6:55–59)

Jesus taught that He is God and came down from heaven. In John 6, He declared that He was virgin born. Even 2,000 years after His return to heaven, all the scientific confirmations of the authenticity of God's Word, and attestations of the millions of individuals with confirmed answers to prayers, skeptics still deny the existence of the Creator.

When our first parents, Adam and Eve, disobeyed God their Creator, He endured immeasurable disappointment. He had created them in His image. The Bible says that in the cool of the day, He would come to spend time communicating with them. Then came the day when God arrived, but neither Adam nor Eve were anywhere to greet Him, as was customary. The text says that "God called unto Adam, and said unto him, "Where *art* thou" (Gen. 3:9, KJV). Then a voice was heard coming from some hiding place.

As they appeared, something was obviously different that day. No longer were they cheerful and happy to see their Maker. On inquiry, God heard their confession: "We heard you coming and hid ourselves because we were naked" (v. 10, personal paraphrase). We should not suppose that

God was not aware of what had occurred. On the contrary, He wanted the pair to admit their sin. Without confession, there would be no repentance, and therefore forgiveness would have served no constructive purpose.

God was more grieved and saddened than angry, though it could be said He was wroth with the provocateur—the devil disguised as a serpent. He asked, "Who told you that you *were* naked" (v. 11)? Sadly, our heavenly Father needed to provide adequate coverage with animal skins for them—something that they were unable to do for themselves. This prefigured a time when Jesus, the Lamb of God, would come to earth as the sacrifice for the sins of all humanity. He would, by His death on the cross, pay the penalty for the transgressions of Adam, Eve, and their posterity.

The first parents realized the high cost of this temporary covering, and that was only the beginning. They had to vacate their beautiful Edenic home, and an angel with a flaming sword was sent to guard the tree of life so that they could not eat its fruit and thereby live forever in their sinful condition. Now their labor would be by sweat and heavy toil; the earth would be dry and hard; the plants would be covered with thorns; and the leaves would wither and die. Death would be the result of all their labors.

God promised them a Deliverer (see v. 15). A Messiah would come at the appropriate time. All this was done for the protection of the human race that God the Creator loved, even in this disappointment. Unknown to them, before the foundation of the world was laid, the triune God made provisions to redeem mankind if they made the wrong choice and sinned. He wants fellowship with His creatures who love and adore Him, but it has to be willingly, not by force. In the entire universe, the only Being who could bring reconciliation between divinity and humanity was God Himself, in the person of His Son.

Preparations were made to bring about this program before the world came into existence. God the Creator undertook to bring about this reconciliation. Death would have to occur to provide the blood necessary for cleansing. There was only one means by which this plan could be effected. Only the gracious and merciful Godhead could accomplish this.

Why did God send Jesus Christ to die for sinners? The mystery of His everlasting love is beyond comprehension. His grace and mercy constitute His response to humanity's sin and rebellion. It is the Father's love that caused Him to send His only Son to die in place of humanity. Why was God willing to do this? John 3:16–17 was His response to mankind's sin. Because Jesus took upon Himself human nature, He was able to give His blood, thus making His perfect life available to those who partake of Him by faith. The life of the flesh is in the blood (see Lev. 17:10–14).

Jesus clothed His divinity in humanity. He was able to live as a man without taking our sinful nature so that by His death He could be a perfect High Priest and advocate for us at the throne of grace. Through His perfect humanity, He could understand our weaknesses, and all who come to Him by faith find in Him sympathy in times of need.

When Jesus claimed to be the bread from heaven, the Jews began to murmur (see John 6:41). When He invited them to eat His flesh, their emotions rose still higher. Some of them saw a deeper meaning in His words than others did, but they all seemed to have been confused by placing too literal a construction on His words.

> *Through His perfect humanity, He could understand our weaknesses, and all who come to Him by faith find in Him sympathy in times of need.*

Jesus' declaration regarding drinking His blood must have shocked His literal-minded hearers (see vs. 52, 53), for the law specifically prohibited the use of blood for consumption (see Gen. 9:4; Deut. 12:16). If the Jews had recalled the reason for this prohibition, they might have better understood the meaning of Jesus' words. The reason given for the prohibition is that the blood is the life. Thus, they might have realized that to eat His flesh and drink His blood means to appropriate His life by faith. "To eat the flesh and drink the blood of Christ is to receive Him as a personal Savior, believing that He forgives our sins, and that we are complete in Him" (White 1898, p. 389).

It is only because Christ gave His human life for us that we may partake of His divine nature. From this, it is clear that to eat His flesh and drink His blood means to believe and have faith in Him. Repeatedly in Scripture, God's love is His answer to mankind's sin and rebellion. He is spoken of as the "living God" (see Deut. 5:26; Matt. 16:16; Acts 14:15; 2 Cor. 6:16).

God is the One who lives of Himself without dependence upon any other being. Thus, He is the source of life for all others in the universe. What is true in this respect of the Father is also true of the Son, for "In Christ is life, original, unborrowed, underived" (White 1898, p. 530). Therefore, the Christian is to be dependent upon Jesus by faith to receive from Him the divine life and nature. It is this life that brings Him forth in the resurrection (see John 1:1–4, 14; 4:13, 14; 5:24–29; 2 Thess. 4:13–18).

As we look at all the devolving changes occurring all over our world, they remind us that Jesus promised that He would come again to take all those who have believed in Him to live with Him in His Father's home in heaven (see John 14:1–3). And we know that He will indeed come again. Today, all over the world, God's messengers are going forth with the message of salvation.

We are reminded of the stubborn willfulness of the people in the days of Noah before the flood, as well as those who lived in Sodom and Gomorrah. In each situation, only a remnant lived by faith in the Son of God. We need to thoughtfully ask ourselves some vital questions every day: 'How is it with me? Am I anchored in Jesus Christ? Am I seeking to love and obey Him daily?' Ready or not, at the Father's appointed time, Jesus will come again, this time not to die, but to reap His harvest and usher in the day of the Lord.

CHAPTER 4

Jesus, His Fulfillment of Prophecy

All the prophecies in the Old Testament concerning the Messiah (approximately 300) found their ultimate fulfillment in Jesus Christ, the Son of God. Many of His teachings seemed contrary to the expectations of the Jewish leaders' understanding of the Messianic prophecies. They expected a kingly Messiah who would drive the Romans from their land, renew the Davidic kingdom, and bring in everlasting peace and righteousness.

As Jesus went about doing good, healing those who were sick in body, mind, and spirit, His popularity grew. His miraculous works were intended to reveal to everyone some of His divine attributes. He raised the dead to life again, cleansed lepers, controlled nature by calming the angry, storm-tossed sea, and walked on the raging waves when He came to His disciples.

As the popularity of the Messiah grew, so also did the leaders resentment of Him. Jesus fed five thousand men, plus women and children, with five small loaves of bread and two small fish. After everyone was filled, the disciples gathered twelve baskets of remaining scraps. When the people saw this miracle, they wanted to make Him king. This was not the purpose of His coming to earth at this time. He came to reveal the love of God and die for the remission of the sins of all who would place their faith and trust in Him.

Jesus could not be the seed of Abraham unless He became a man, and He could not be the Savior of mankind unless He was God. He is the Angel of the Lord mentioned many times in the Old Testament. He claimed divine authority, exercised divine prerogatives, and received homage and worship. Since, therefore, we find these terms are not applied to different angels indiscriminately, but to One in particular, and the work attributed to this Angel is elsewhere attributed to God Himself, it is certain that the Angel of the Lord in the early books of Scripture refers to a divine person distinct from the Father.

Elsewhere in Scripture, we also find the express testimony of the inspired writers of the New Testament that the Angel of the Lord, who led the Israelites through the wilderness and dwelt in the temple, was Christ. That is, the Angel was the Word, the Eternal Son of God who became flesh and fulfilled the work that was predicted the Messiah should accomplish.

The apostles did not hesitate to apply to Christ Old Testament language used to set forth the majesty, works, and kingdom of Jehovah (see John 12:41; Rom. 14:11; 1 Cor. 10:4; Heb. 1:10–13). Therefore, the New Testament clearly identifies the Word—the Son of God—with the Angel of the Lord and Messenger of the Covenant of the Old Testament. The Angel who appeared to Hagar, Abraham, Moses, Joshua, Gideon, and others, was called Jehovah and worshipped as Adonai. He claimed divine homage and exercised divine power, was set forth as the Son of God, Wonderful Counselor, and Prince of Peace, and predicted to be born of a virgin by the psalmists and prophets. The One to whom every knee should bow and tongue confess is none other than our Lord and Savior, Jesus Christ.

> *Jesus could not be the seed of Abraham unless He became a man, and He could not be the Savior of mankind unless He was God.*

> Why do the heathen rage, and the people imagine a vain thing? The kings of the earth set themselves, and the rulers take counsel together, against the LORD, and against

his anointed, *saying*, Let us break their bands asunder, and cast away their cords from us. He that sitteth in the heavens shall laugh: the Lord shall have them in derision. Then shall he speak unto them in his wrath, and vex them in his sore displeasure. Yet have I set my king upon my holy hill of Zion. I will declare the decree: the LORD hath said unto me, Thou *art* my Son; this day have I begotten thee. (Psalm 2:1–7, KJV)

Psalm 22:19–21 reflects a sufferer's words that our Lord appropriated to Himself when on the cross. This sufferer prays for deliverance. The results of that deliverance prove that the Person must be divine. His sufferings and deliverance make it definite that all faithful people will fear and love God for having rescued Him from His enemies. As a result, nations will be converted to God, and blessings which He secures will last forever.

We also find that Psalm 72 describes an exalted King and the blessings of His reign. These passages are of such a nature that it seems evident that their subject must be a divine person. His kingdom is to be everlasting and universal, and will provide perfect peace with God and goodwill to humanity. Through love, all mankind will submit to Him. In Him, all nations of the earth are to be blessed, as we are taught in Galatians 3:13–14.

Psalm 110 is frequently quoted in the New Testament and applied to Jesus Christ to present the dignity of His person and the nature of His work. He is David's Lord. With that being the case, how then can He be David's Son? Jesus posed this question, in so many words, to the Pharisees to convince them that their ideas about the Messiah did not measure up to their interpretation of the Scriptures. He was indeed to be David's Son as the expected Messiah, yet at the same time, He possessed a nature that made Him David's Lord.

In keeping with His divine nature, He was to sit at the Father's right hand, associated with Him regarding equality in glory and dominion. Such is the apostle's exposition of the aforementioned psalm in Hebrews 1:13.

God has never said to any other person except Christ, "Sit on My right hand." The Subject of this psalm is no mere creature, but the *Logos*—the Word of God—and Creator of all things (see John 1:1–4, 14).

This Person who is simultaneously David's Son and David's Lord is eternally both Priest and King. Hebrews 7:17 indicates that His priesthood is not in the Aaronic line but after the order of Melchizedek. In Psalm 110:1–5 He is declared to be the Supreme Lord, for He is called *Adonai*, a title that is reserved for only the true and living God.

What does the prophet say? Isaiah 4:2 predicted the coming of the Branch of Jehovah. His advent would bring pardon from sin, purification, and perfect security, as well as prove Him to be an everlasting, divine person. Isaiah 6 records the prophet's vision of Jehovah in His holy temple, surrounded by hosts of angels who worship Him day and night. John 12:41 refers to Isaiah's said vision and alludes to Christ being the center thereof.

Do you know Jesus? If not, get to know Him, for your life will be forever changed, radically and for the better.

> For unto us a child is born, unto us a son is given: and the government shall be upon his shoulder: and his name shall be called Wonderful, Counsellor, The mighty God, The everlasting Father, The Prince of Peace. Of the increase of *his* government and peace *there shall be* no end, upon the throne of David, and upon his kingdom, to order it, and to establish it with judgment and with justice from henceforth even for ever. The zeal of the LORD of hosts will perform this. (Isaiah 9:6, 7, KJV)

The results of His earthly advent and dominion only flow from the throne of God. In Isaiah 11, we find another description of the perfection of this Person and His kingdom. Chapters 40 through 66 include many more prophetic accounts of the Messiah. The coming of the Messiah would affect the redemption of His people from Babylonian captivity. He would secure their pardon from sin and bring about reconciliation with God the Father and the prevalence of true religion throughout the earth.

Micah 5:1–5 predicted the birth of One who was to be born in Bethlehem Ephrathah, the city of David. There was another Bethlehem in the northern region of the country. He would be the ruler of Israel, the people of God. He was to be born of a virgin, though He has existed eternally. He shall rule in the strength and majesty of God, and His government shall show forth the attributes of glory. His dominion shall be universal. The effect of His kingdom shall be peace—perfect harmony, order, and blessedness.

Jeremiah 23 speaks of the restoration of the kingdom of God on the earth among all His people. This was to be brought about by One who is declared to be a descendant of David. He would be called the "Branch," a designation that links this prophecy with those of Isaiah 4 and 11. He was to be a king, and His reign was to be prosperous. Judah and Israel were to be united again in perfect harmony, and peace was to be secured. Daniel 2:44 predicted that the kingdom of the Messiah would supersede and absorb all other earthly kingdoms and last forever.

Today, many people see Jesus as a good teacher and Jewish seer who suffered an unjust and cruel death. One of the strangest occurrences is to meet someone who professes not to know who Jesus Christ is. He made the boldest claims about His identity: "Most assuredly, I say to you, before Abraham was, I Am" (John 8:58). Those who heard Him became incensed and attempted to throw stones at Him, but He walked through their midst and escaped. His hour had not yet come.

On another occasion, the people asked:

> "If You are the Christ, tell us plainly." Jesus answered them, "I told you, and you do not believe. The works that I do in My Father's name, they bear witness of Me. But you do not believe, because you are not of My sheep, as I said to you. My sheep hear my voice, and I know them,

and they follow Me. And I give them eternal life, and they shall never perish; neither shall anyone snatch them out of My hand. My Father, who has given *them* to Me, is greater than all; and no one is able to snatch *them* out of My Father's hand. I and *My* Father are One." (John 10:24–30)

That is to say, the Father and Jesus are both divine. Jesus, on many occasions, confirmed His identity (e.g., John 5:17, 18). One could not reasonably misunderstand the implication of what He said. After He uttered the words quoted in the passage above, they again picked up stones to stone Him. God the Father and Jesus are both divine. They have existed from eternity and are self-existent beings.

Jesus Christ claimed authority to forgive sins (see Mark 2:5–11). The scribes understood that He was claiming a prerogative that belongs only to God. Yahweh is the one pictured in the Old Testament who alone forgives sin (see Jer. 31:34).

Jesus claimed to have the power to raise the dead (see John 11:25). Regarding Lazarus, who had been embalmed and buried for four days:

Jesus said to her, "Your brother will rise again." Martha said to Him, "I know that he will rise again in the resurrection at the last day." Jesus said to her, "I am the resurrection and the life. He who believes in Me, though he may die, he shall live. And whoever lives and believes in Me shall never die. Do you believe this?" She said to Him, "Yes, Lord, I believe that You are the Christ, the Son of God, who is to come into the world." ...Then Jesus, again groaning in Himself, came to the tomb. It was a cave, and a stone lay against it. Jesus said, "Take away the stone." Martha, the sister of him who was dead, said to Him, "Lord, by this time there is a stench, for he has been *dead* four days." Jesus said to her, "Did I not say to you that if you would believe you would see the glory of God?" Then they took away the stone *from the place* where the dead man was lying. And Jesus lifted up *His* eyes and said, "Father, I thank You that You have heard Me. And I know that You always hear Me, but because of the people who are standing by I said *this,* that they may believe that You sent Me." Now when He had said these things, He cried with a loud voice, "Lazarus, come forth!" And he who had died came out bound hand and foot with graveclothes, and his face was wrapped with a cloth. Jesus said to them, "Loose him, and let him go." (John 11:23–27, 38–44)

By these miracles, Jesus demonstrated His divinity. Additionally, He stated, "[A]ll should honor the Son just as they honor the Father" (5:23). On many occasions, He received worship without forbidding such actions (see Matt. 8:2; 9:18; 14:33; 28:9, 17; Mark 5:6; John 9:38). He has instructed us to pray in His name: "If you ask anything in My name, I will do *it*" (John 14:14).

Of Jesus, Paul the apostle stated, "Therefore God also has highly exalted Him and given Him the name which is above every name, that at the name of Jesus every knee should bow, of those in heaven, and of those on earth, and of those under the earth, and *that* every tongue should confess that Jesus Christ *is* Lord, to the glory of God the Father" (Phil. 2:9–11). By this, he is telling us that the Father is upholding the fact that Jesus Christ is God by exalting His name to the level of the One through whom we make our requests and before whom we bow.

Jesus also assures us that He will be the One who will give answers to our prayers. "And in that day you will ask Me nothing. Most assuredly, I say to you, whatever you ask the Father in My name He will give you. Until now you have asked nothing in My name. Ask, and you will receive, that your joy may be full" (John 16:23, 24). Also, "And whatever you ask in My name, that I will do, that the Father may be glorified in the Son.... If you love Me, keep My commandments" (14:13, 15).

Jesus claimed to have the power that only God alone possesses—to raise and judge the dead.

> "Most assuredly, I say to you, the hour is coming, and now is, when the dead will hear the voice of the Son of God; and those who hear will live.... all who are in the graves will hear His voice and come forth—those who have done good, to the resurrection of life, and those who have done evil, to the resurrection of condemnation. I can of myself do nothing. As I hear, I judge; and My judgment is righteous, because I do not seek My own will but the will of the Father who sent Me." (John 5:25, 28–30)

Christ claimed to hold people's eternal destiny (see John 6:47, 54.) The book of Hebrews is most emphatic that Jesus is God. Paul quoted Psalm 45:6. "But to the Son *He says*: "Your throne, O God, *is* forever and ever; A scepter of righteousness *is* the scepter of Your kingdom" (1:8).

The late, renowned Christian writer, C. S. Lewis, observed, "I am trying here to prevent anyone saying the really foolish thing that people often say about Him: I'm ready to accept Jesus as a great moral teacher..." (*Mere Christianity*). The Bible predicted the exact year and place of the Messiah's arrival to earth. In Daniel 9:25, the angel Gabriel came to the prophet approximately 580 years before the event came to pass and told him: "Know therefore and understand, *That* from the going forth of the command To restore and build Jerusalem Until Messiah the Prince, *There shall be* seven weeks and sixty-two weeks."

Daniel had been studying the prophecies of Jeremiah. Therefore, he was concerned about his nation and the city of Jerusalem. Jeremiah's prophecy had revealed that the Jews were to be in Babylon for seventy years from the time when they had been taken captive and by King Nebuchadnezzar. Regarding Daniel 9:25, King Artaxerxes 7 issued decrees to Ezra the Jewish scribe, not in 445 BC or 444 BC, as some interpreters conclude, but in 457 BC.

This, then, would be the date for the start of the seventy-week prophecy. "Seventy weeks are determined upon thy people" (v. 24, KJV). The word "determined" is *chathak* (kah—'thak) in Hebrew and has been variously translated as "determined," "decreed," "divided," and "cut off." This period of seventy prophetic weeks, or 490 literal years, is to be separated from the longer period of 2,300 prophetic days, or literal years. This is the longest prophecy in the Word of God. This 490-day/year-period that was allotted to the Jewish nation would take us to AD 27. Precisely on time, the Messiah appeared and was anointed. Jesus came to John the Baptist and asked to be baptized.

Jesus was the spotless, sinless Lamb of God. Therefore, one may appropriately ask, "If that is true, why would the Messiah need to be baptized?" John the Baptist protested, telling Christ that he was the one who needed to be baptized by Him. Jesus insisted, then gave us the reason why he should baptize Him.

> The next day John saw Jesus coming toward him, and said, "Behold! The Lamb of God who takes away the sin of the world! This is He of whom I said, 'After me comes a Man who is preferred before me, for He was before me.' I did not know Him; but that He should be revealed to Israel, therefore I came baptizing with water." And John bore witness, saying, "I saw the Spirit descending from heaven like a dove, and He remained upon Him. I did not know Him, but He who sent me to baptize with water said to me, 'Upon whom you see the Spirit descending, and remaining on Him, this is He who baptizes with the Holy Spirit.' And I have seen and testified that this is the Son of God" Again, the next day, John stood with two of his disciples. And looking at Jesus as He walked, he said, "Behold the Lamb of God!" The two disciples heard him speak, and they followed Jesus. (John 1:29–37; see also Exodus 12:3; 1 Peter 1:19; Isaiah 53:11; 1 John 2:12)

The third decree issued in 457 BC by Artaxerxes (see Ezra 7:11–26) starts the 490-year period that culminates in Christ's earthly ministry. Daniel 9:25–27 foretold not only the appearance and ministry of the Messiah but also His death. As documented earlier, Jesus was baptized as an example to everyone. The Jewish people, during the time of the Lord's earthly ministry, were definitely acquainted with Daniel's prophecies. They knew He was to be born in Bethlehem Ephrathah (Matt. 2:3–6).

No fewer than twenty-nine prophecies were fulfilled in the twenty-four-hour period leading to Jesus' crucifixion and death on Calvary. Here is a dozen of them:

- The Passover lambs were slain on the fourteenth day of the first month (see Ex. 12:3–6; Lev. 23:5) were vivid depictions of the Messiah's sacrifice, although at the time the Israelites never fully understood it. Passover was first introduced in Egypt on the last night before they left.
- It was on this same day of the Hebrew calendar that Jesus was crucified.
- "They pierced My hands and My feet" (Ps. 22:16). This prophecy described a form of execution that was not known when David wrote this passage—almost 800 years before crucifixion was adopted by the Romans.
- "[T]hey will look upon Mw whom they have pierced" (Zech. 12:10). The beloved apostle recorded this verse's fulfillment (see John 19:34–37).
- "He guards all his bones; Not one of them is broken" (Ps. 34:20). "But when they came to Jesus and saw that He was already dead, they did not break His legs.... For these things were done that the Scripture should be fulfilled, 'Not *one* of His bones shall be broken'" (John 19:33, 36; see also Num. 9:12).
- "They divide My garments among them, And for My clothing they cast lots" (Ps. 22:18; see John 19:23, 24).
- He would pray for His executioners (see Isa. 53:12).
- Jesus prayed, "Father, forgive them, for they do not know what they do" (Luke 23:34).

- He would be executed with criminals (see Isa. 53:12). Jesus was crucified between two thieves (see Matt. 27:38).
- It was prophesied that Jesus would be forsaken by His followers. This prophecy was fulfilled when Jesus was arrested. His disciples, fearing for their safety, all ran away to hide. "Strike the Shepherd, And the sheep will be scattered" (Zech. 13:7).
- He would be betrayed by His trusted friend. Judas Iscariot, one of His disciples, sold Him for the price of a slave—thirty pieces of silver—to the chief priests and rabbis. "Even my own familiar friend in whom I trusted, Who ate my bread, Has lifted up *his* heel against me" (Ps. 41:9). "And they counted out to him thirty pieces of silver. So from that time [Judas] sought opportunity to betray Him" (Matt. 26:15, 16).
- Jesus was offered vinegar and gall to drink. On the cross, Jesus said, "I thirst" and they gave Him the mingled beverage. However, when He had tasted it, He refused to drink it (see Matt. 27:34; Ps. 69:21).

> *The sheer number of these prophecies, and the precision of their fulfillment, all point to one person—Jesus of Nazareth, the Lamb of God, destined to be slain to redeem us before the foundation of the world.*

The sheer number of these prophecies, and the precision of their fulfillment, all point to one person—Jesus of Nazareth, the Lamb of God, destined to be slain to redeem us before the foundation of the world. God, who can control all things, prompted all these prophecies to be written hundreds of years before they were fulfilled on time. Simon Peter said, "[T]hose things which God foretold by the mouth of all His prophets, that the Christ would suffer, He has thus fulfilled" (Acts 3:18). Paul reaffirmed "that Christ died for our sins according to the Scriptures" (1 Cor. 15:3).

Who has believed our report? And to whom has the arm of the LORD been revealed? For He shall grow up before Him as a tender plant, And as a root out of dry ground. He has no form or comeliness; And when we see Him, *There is* no beauty that we should desire Him. He is despised and rejected by men, A man of sorrows and acquainted with grief. And we hid, as it were, *our* faces from Him; He was despised, and we did not esteem Him. Surely He has borne our griefs And carried our sorrows; Yet we esteemed Him stricken, Smitten by God, and afflicted. But he *was* wounded for our transgressions, *He was* bruised for our iniquities; The chastisement for our peace *was* upon Him, And by His stripes we are healed. All we like sheep have gone astray; We have turned, every one, to his own way; And the LORD has laid on Him the iniquity of us all. He was oppressed and He was afflicted, Yet he opened not His mouth; He was led as a lamb to the slaughter, And as a sheep before its shearers is silent, So He opened not His mouth. He was taken from prison and from judgment, And who will declare His generation? For he was cut off from the land of the living; For the transgressions of My people He was stricken. And they made His grave with the wicked—But with the rich at His death, Because He had done no violence, Nor *was any* deceit in His mouth. Yet it pleased the LORD to bruise Him; He has put *Him* to grief. When you make His soul an offering for sin, He shall see *His* seed, He shall prolong *His* days, And the pleasure of the LORD shall prosper in His hand. He shall see the labor of His soul, *and* be satisfied. By His knowledge My righteous Servant shall justify many, For He shall bear their iniquities. Therefore I will divide Him a portion with the great, And He shall divide the spoil with the strong, Because He poured out His soul unto death, And

He was numbered with the transgressors, And He bore the sin of many, And made intercession for the transgressors. (Isaiah 53:1–12)

C. Mervyn Maxwell, in his book *God Cares* (vol. 1) tells us that:

The date of the cross was foretold ... Is there any evidence that Jesus' death occurred in the year that we calculated it would, that is, in A.D. 31? ... All commentators take into account that the crucifixion occurred, in general, while Pontius Pilate was procurator [of Judea] (A.D. 26–36) and, in particular, at a Passover that fell no more than three or four years later than His baptism. ... Daniel 9 indicates that the interval between the Messiah's anointing (at His baptism) and the time of His death would be **"half of the week,"** or three and a half years. The Gospel of John, by recording the annual Passovers that Jesus attended, provides evidence that three and a half years did elapse between the baptism of Christ and His death.

John 2 and 3 tell about a Passover during which Jesus talked at night with Nicodemus and told him that he must be born again.

John 5:1 tells of a feast, most probably a Passover, in connection with which Jesus healed a man who had suffered thirty-eight years from paralysis.

John 6:4 tells of a Passover season during which Jesus fed a very large crowd with a boy's small lunch.

John 12:1 introduces the Passover season during which Jesus died.

We have seen that Christ's baptism occurred near the end of A.D. 27. So His first (or "Nicodemus") Passover occurred in the spring of A.D. 28. Then his second (or "paralytic") Passover fell in the spring of A.D. 29, His third (or "large-meal") Passover came in the spring of A.D. 30—and His final (or "crucifixion") Passover occurred three and a half years after His baptism, that is to say, *in the spring of A.D. 31,* just as [the angel] Gabriel had indicated.

If Gabriel were an athlete instead of an angel, we would stand to our feet and cheer!

Gabriel's dependability reminds us that according to Daniel 9:24 one of the purposes of the seventy weeks was to **"*seal* up the vision and prophecy"** (K.J.V.) of the 2300 days. Because the shorter prophecy was so stunningly fulfilled, we have reason to depend on the longer one.

Of course, what Jesus *did* during the seventieth week accomplished far more than chronology ever could to seal the vision and prophecy. (pp. 218–219)

"LORD, who shall abide in thy tabernacle? who shall dwell in thy holy hill? He that walketh uprightly, and worketh righteousness, and speaketh the truth in his heart.... *He that* sweareth to *his own* hurt, and changeth not" (Ps. 15:1, 2, 4).

In all of history, only One perfectly kept His promises, no matter how much pain He would have to endure, and that One was Jesus. In Gethsemane, stretched out on the ground in agony the night before the cross, He pleaded with God the Father to find a simpler way to save the human race. In His humanity, He did not want to be crucified, yet in the divinely ordained plan, He knew that He was the only One in the entire universe capable and qualified to save the human race from sin's everlasting night. It was for this purpose that He had come to earth's darkest regions. Yes, for this He came, and He would not now recant. His redeeming love for sinners allowed no other course of action. He would go to the cross to reclaim sinners. All who will come to Him will rest from the torment of sin and find rest. If you were the only one who had strayed, our Savior would have gone into the chasm of hell to redeem just you.

Crucifixion was an excessively brutal way to die. The Romans reserved it for traitors, robbers, and most of all, slaves. They conducted it publicly for the deterrent effect. They stripped a convict naked and flogged him until His chest and back were shredded. Then they arranged his legs in an uncomfortable position and drove blunt nails through his ankles and wrists into a wooden frame.

For Jesus, even far more distressing than the torture of crucifixion was His separation from the Father. In poignant anguish on the cross, He shouted, "My God, My God, why hast thou forsaken me" (Matt. 27:46, KJV)? The Father did not actually forsake His Son (see John 16:32). However, to be our substitute and Savior, He, in some mysterious manner, had to experience the dreadful torment that all impenitent sinners will suffer in the judgment—that final penalty when they realize that, by their own choice in forsaking Jesus, they are lost forever.

In order to save us, Christ identified Himself with us. "For he hath made him *to be* sin for us, who knew no sin; that we might be made the righteousness of God in him" (2 Cor. 5:21, KJV). James Moffatt, in his translation, phrased the previous verse as follows.: "For our sakes [God] made [Christ] to be sin who himself knew nothing of sin, so that in him we might become the righteousness of God."

Jesus, on the cross, sensed Himself being separated like a sinner from His Father. This separation, this ugly alienation, was to Him utterly horrendous and heart-rending. Our Intercessor now longed for an intercessor of His own. On the cross, His prayer now breathed submission: "[N]ot as I will, but as Thou wilt" (Matt. 26:39). He would keep His promise. He would die for humanity, though even His best friends did not care enough to stay awake with Him.

> *In all of history, only One perfectly kept His promises, no matter how much pain He would have to endure, and that One was Jesus.*

Jesus is a promise-keeping Savior and covenant-keeping God. Daniel 9:27 foretold that He would conduct Himself in this way. He ratified the promise at all cost to Himself, then applied it to even the most wicked sinner who sought out its benefits. The Messiah would keep His promise, no matter what. This is the last of the seventy weeks allotted to the Jewish people. It was to come after the sixty-nine weeks. In the middle of the final week, Jesus was to cause sacrifices and oblations to cease. That is, three and a half years after His anointing, He was to be killed.

The Bible record shows that He did this. A few hours before He chose to die, an unruly mob shouted angrily, "His blood be on us, and on our children" (Matt. 27:25). About seven weeks after the cross, on the day of Pentecost, Simon Peter, citing the promise of God, offered forgiveness to these same people and their same children. "Repent, and be baptized every one of you in the name of Jesus Christ for the remission of sins, and ye shall receive the gift of the Holy Ghost. For the promise is unto you, and to your children, and to all that are afar off, *even* as many as the Lord our God shall call" (Acts 2:38, 39, KJV).

Thus, in the years following the cross, thousands of Jews accepted the threefold benefits of the new covenant: 1) Forgiveness of every sin, 2) Power to live changed lives, and 3) Membership in God's family—people who, from every nation, tribe, and language, would accept His salvation full and free. This new covenant is for all who will come to God through Jesus Christ, His Son, who beckons, "Come unto Me, all *ye* that labour and are heavy laden, and I will give you rest. Take my yoke upon you, and learn of me" (Matt. 11:28, 29, KJV).

God, in Christ, is making this free offer because of His love for us. "For God so loved the world that He gave His only begotten Son, that whoever believes in Him should not perish but have everlasting life. For God did not send His Son into the world to condemn the world, but that the world through Him might be saved" (John 3:16, 17). Each person who accepts this promise has God's full assurance through His Son Jesus Christ because of Calvary, and thus stands redeemed.

CHAPTER 5

Strength Through Suffering

At the very beginning of his first epistle, Simon Peter identified himself as an apostle of Jesus Christ. An apostle is one who is sent with a message. Other similar terms are "ambassador," "emissary," and "representative," meaning "one who speaks for another." The letter is addressed to God's elect and chosen. Peter describes those to whom he wrote as strangers scattered or dispersed abroad and aliens and strangers in a foreign land. Those to whom he wrote included both Jewish and Gentile Christians living outside Jerusalem. They were scattered abroad because of persecution, in an area located mainly in northern Turkey.

The main reason for Peter's letter was to encourage them to hold fast to the profession of their faith in Jesus. He attributed their being scattered abroad to God's foreknowledge. This thought suggests that all we go through is according to our heavenly Father's care and the sanctifying work of the Holy Spirit, who turns every circumstance in our lives—every joy, burden, sorrow, and hardship—into a means of spiritual maturing. He sees every teardrop, grief, and obstacle that crosses our pathway and uses it to foster growth and preparation for heaven.

> *This thought suggests that all we go through is according to our heavenly Father's care and the sanctifying work of the Holy Spirit, who turns every circumstance in our lives—every joy, burden, sorrow, and hardship—into a means of spiritual maturing. He sees every teardrop, grief, and obstacle that crosses our pathway and uses it to foster growth and preparation for heaven.*

Peter wrote that all we endure here in this life is according to our heavenly Father's loving care. Now I need to clarify a potential misunderstanding. Please take what I am about to say to mind and heart. Often, when some disaster, sickness, or accident crosses our pathway, many immediately blame God. Friend, that is a gross mistake. That is the last thing He would send our way. However, sometimes He may allow these situations to occur and use them to strengthen our faith in Him and develop our spiritual stamina.

We need to understand that no matter the trials and sorrows we experience, God can bring some good out of them. The Christian's journey is a walk of faith. When situations come our way, we can look to Jesus Christ, and though the trek will sometimes get difficult, our heavenly Father, through the power of His Holy Spirit, uses these circumstances to make us stronger. Let's look to our Great High Priest at the throne. He traveled that road before we did and will lighten the load. Just trust Him.

God is not the One to blame. An enemy has done this, and nothing pleases Satan more than to hear us blame the Lord for the mischiefs he has committed. Turn to Job 1 and 2. The devil brings difficult situations our way and giggles when God gets the blame. If instead of wrongfully blaming our Savior, we draw closer to Him and ask for help, He will grant us more filling of His Holy Spirit. As we draw closer to our heavenly Father, He gives us more strength to bear the burden of suffering. Jesus suffered far more than any of us ever could and will help us overcome.

Christian friend, Jesus walked this way before us and promised that He will help us walk it also. Sometimes we cannot seem to understand; perhaps we may never know the reason. Just keep walking by faith, One day soon, Jesus will make it plain to us, and then we will understand.

Peter wrote about the believers' relationship with God the Father, and his opening words are worshipful praise:

> Blessed *be* the God and Father of our Lord Jesus Christ, who according to His abundant mercy has begotten us again to a living hope through the resurrection of Jesus Christ from the dead, to an inheritance incorruptible and undefiled and that does not fade away, reserved in heaven for you, who are kept by the power of God through faith for salvation ready to be revealed in the last time" (1 Peter 1:3–5).

The final clause is a reference to the return of Jesus Christ. In this same thought, Peter speaks of being obedient to our Lord and Savior. Obedience carries the idea of being attentive to what we hear from above. It implies a change of conduct on the part of the believer, which involves listening and submitting to God. In this context, since we are chosen by Him and objects of His paternal care, we are never out of His plan for us.

That spirit of obedience begins with accepting Jesus as our personal Lord and Savior and continues by living each day as He told us to live, by the power of the Holy Spirit. We, therefore, obey His call to salvation in Him in the framework of our daily, personal relationship (see Matt. 11:28–30; John 15:4–9).

For Christians, the blood that Christ shed on the cross covers all our sins and bring us salvation. To those who are sprinkled with His blood and obedient to Him, Peter gave the greeting, "Grace… and peace…" This reflects the typical Hebrew wish for wholeness and a meaningful life, which is God's free, undeserved grace that each person receives each day.

Peter linked our position in salvation's history to what he calls a "living hope" (1:3). Our hope is a living hope because it finds its basis in the resurrection of Jesus Christ from the dead. Because He lives, we have the assurance that, abiding in Him, we will also live eternally. Peter called it "an inheritance incorruptible and undefiled," and this emphasizes the believers' eternal inheritance in heaven, unmarred by sin, death, or anything evil, "and that does not fade away."

Our inheritance in Christ is sin-proof, death-proof, time-proof, and imperishable. It is kept (reserved) in heaven by God for believers (see v. 4). A prophet tells us that Jesus is going to make an utter end of sin, for "Affliction will not rise up a second time" (Nah. 1:9). Regardless of how long or what form these trials assume, the length is not to be counted in the light of eternity. Our relationship with our heavenly Father, as we grow more like Christ, is a foretaste of what salvation will be like when He returns.

Why does God allow suffering? He does so to prove if our faith is genuine. His followers, in both the Old and New Testaments, knew that He used trying situations to test their hearts, that they might grow and mature spiritually. God's purposes for present circumstances may not be known for some time, or even in this lifetime at all. However, He has promised that He will make all things plain to us someday, and He is a promise-keeping Father.

> In this you greatly rejoice, though now for a little while, if need be, you have been grieved by various trials, that the genuineness of your faith, *being* much more precious than gold that perishes, though it is tested by fire, may be found to praise, honor, and glory at the revelation of Jesus Christ, whom having not seen you love. Though now you do not see *Him,* yet believing, you rejoice with joy inexpressible and full of glory, receiving the end of your faith—the salvation of *your* souls. Of this salvation the prophets have inquired and searched carefully, who prophesied of the grace *that would come* to you, searching what, or what manner of time, the Spirit of Christ who was in them was indicating when He testified beforehand the sufferings of Christ and the glories that would follow. To them it was revealed that, not to themselves, but to us they were ministering the things which now have been reported to you through those who have preached the gospel to you by the Holy Spirit sent from heaven—things which angels desire to look into. (1 Peter 1:6–12)

If only we could grasp the blessings of salvation supplied by God through Jesus Christ, about which angelic beings are anxious to learn. Every time I read Peter's words, my spirit is uplifted, knowing that the prophets and angels were immensely curious about this great mystery God kept hidden from eternity regarding planet earth and its inhabitants. For those who would believe His love for humanity, the mystery continued, even to the coming of Christ and His redemptive crucifixion. Such a great sacrifice! "How shall we escape, if we neglect so great salvation" (Heb. 2:3, KJV)? If we refuse His sacrifice, there will be no more solution for sin, but instead, only a fearful looking forward to His judgment.

Old Testament prophets did not understand the timing or calendar of dates surrounding the incarnation of Jesus Christ. They did not understand that their words would have a dramatic impact on future generations.

They realized that the things about which they wrote were not for their time, but for those who would live in later eras, hear the gospel, and follow the Savior (see Heb. 11:32, 36–39). For centuries, they faithfully recorded their prophecies about the coming Messiah, even though they did not know who He would be or when He would come to earth.

Even the angels in heaven were looking intently to see if they could get a glimpse of the grace of God at work. We too, in our day, have received that same grace in the Person of Jesus Christ our Lord. We are the heirs and beneficiaries of the full message of the prophets. This is why Paul wrote, "All Scripture *is* given by inspiration of God, and *is* profitable for doctrine, for reproof, for correction, for instruction in righteousness, that the man of God may be complete, thoroughly equipped for every good work" (2 Tim. 3:16, 17).

In 1 Peter 1:13–25, we will see why it is imperative that, as followers of Christ, we submit ourselves to the Holy Spirit's control, so that Christ will live out His life through us. Thus, a watching world will witness that we are His disciples. He said, "A new commandment I give to you, that you love one another; as I have loved you, that you also love one another. By this all will know that you are My disciples, if you have love for one another" (John 13:34, 35).

Peter set the boundaries for our behavior as followers of Christ. The word "Therefore" in 1:13 points back to the preceding discussion that dealt with our eternal hope in Christ. That hope became a reality to us when we surrendered ourselves to the Lord. First, believers are to live each day with their focus fixed on the day of His return, whenever that day may be. The phrase "at the revelation of Jesus Christ" directs our attention to an undisclosed future day when He will return as He promised. Believers are to live each day looking forward to that final day.

We are to harness our thoughts, even as we live lives fully surrendered to Jesus, by the power of the Holy Spirit. As we bring our thoughts into harmony with the will of God, He will assist us in not allowing situations to become distractions. We are to hold fast to Jesus, the Author and Finisher of our faith. In verses 10 through 12, Peter attempted to increase our appreciation for the great salvation that we enjoy in Christ. The spiritual blessings we experience are grander than anything the Old Testament prophets, or even the angels, could have imagined.

Oh yes, the prophets longed to participate in this salvation plan and understand the grace of God more fully. They researched the subject as thoroughly as they could in an effort to comprehend that which we today take for granted. They understood and wrote that the Messiah must first suffer, but they did not understand it clearly. Our suffering is not a sign that God has forsaken us. It is a sign of our fellowship with Christ our Redeemer. After the suffering, the rewards and glory will follow.

"To them it was revealed that, not to themselves but to us they were ministering the things which now have been reported to you through those who have preached the gospel to you by the Holy Spirit sent from heaven—things which angels desire to look into" (v. 12). Wow! We must dare not forget the beginning of our great salvation. Neither should we forget the end. We must keep our minds clear for action and stay alert.

This means that we must be self-controlled and be spiritually aware, as well as mindful about what we face in life, especially when we are undergoing trials and suffering. Simon Peter cautioned, "[G]ird up the loins of your mind, be sober, and rest *your* hope fully upon the grace that is to be brought to you at the revelation of Jesus Christ; as obedient children, not conforming yourselves to the former lusts, *as* in your ignorance; but as He who called you *is* holy, you also be holy in all *your* conduct, because it is written, 'Be holy, for I am holy'" (vs. 13–16; ref. Lev. 11:45).

Both the Old and New Testaments have more to say about the holiness of God than any of His other attributes. According to the instructions in His Word, He requires us to be holy, even as He is holy. The intended meaning is that just we, as believers, seek to promote and develop Christian hope, we must also cultivate personal holiness. Holiness may be expressed as differentiation or distinction and includes a specific, moral sense of separation from evil and dedication to a life of right living.

The lives and attitudes of Christians should be different in quality because of their relationship with Jesus. Holiness produces in our lives loving conformity to God's commands, which then generates, in sincere followers, Christ's character. He is concerned with individual actions and the motives that impel them.

> And if you call on the Father, who without partiality judges according to each one's work, conduct yourselves throughout the time of your stay *here* in fear; knowing that you were not redeemed with corruptible things, *like* silver or gold, from your aimless conduct *received* by tradition from your fathers, but with the precious blood of Christ, as of a lamb without blemish and without spot. He indeed was foreordained before the foundation of the world, but was manifest in these times for you who through Him believe in God, who raised Him from the dead and gave Him glory, so that your faith and hope are in God. (1 Peter 1:17–21).

God is not partial. He is the Creator of all mankind and treats each person equally. He is going to judge every person's work one day, and this fact ought to cause us to live soberly in this evil world. This has everything to do with the kind of life each person has been living down here. If we are superficial in our interactions with others, God sees us and judges accordingly.

The gospel transforms and changes our lives for the better. Believers have their very existence from the living Savior, who is now in heaven interceding on our behalf at the throne of grace. We were not redeemed with gold or silver, but rather the precious blood of Jesus, the Lamb without spot or blemish. God is unchanging, and His immutability is the terror of the wicked if they even give it any thought. With that said, a day of judgment is coming when all must give an account of their deeds to Him.

"Seeing you have purified your souls in obeying the truth through the Spirit unto unfeigned love of the brethren, *see that ye* love one another with a pure heart fervently" (v. 22, KJV). Peter emphasized this point, perhaps remembering the language that Jesus used with him years earlier.

God demands that we relate to one another with self-sacrificing love. This is a kind of love that a person must work at developing, even when life is difficult. The love we extend to one another must be constant and enduring, unshaken by adversity or painful circumstances.

The new birth and the communication thereof are brought about through the agency and instrument of the Word of God, which includes the Old and New Testament Scriptures, especially the apostolic proclamation of the gospel message. "[H]aving been born again, not of corruptible seed but incorruptible, through the word of God which lives and abides forever, because 'All flesh *is* as grass, And all the glory of man as the flower of the grass. The grass withers, and its flower falls away, But the word of the Lord endures forever.' Now this is the word which by the gospel was preached to you" (vs. 23–25).

The Word of God stands as the foundation of the proclamation of the gospel of salvation through Jesus Christ. This is demonstrated by our love for others—His love acted out in our lives. God is in the business of giving us a hope and future. The Bible is central in the life of the believer, and the death and resurrection of Jesus Christ form

Our outward life will only change if it is a natural outworking of an inner change.

the bedrock of one's redemption. Any sound theology of His second coming must emphasize the positive behavior that is to mark the Christian way of life today.

Examine your life daily for genuine marks of holiness and obedience to Jesus Christ, and cultivate reverential awe toward God. He is worthy of all worship, adulation, and praise. Our outward life will only change if it is a natural outworking of an inner change. Reverence undergirds the believer's desire to live a life of holiness and obedience, even in the face of difficulties. We are to walk by faith in Jesus and conform to His example as God's suffering Servant.

CHAPTER 6

Jesus Paid Our Sin-Debt with His Blood

I cherish the opening words of a particular hymn: "There is a fountain filled with blood, drawn from Immanuel's veins; and sinners plunged beneath that flood, lose all their guilty stains." "In that day there shall be a fountain opened to the house of David and to the inhabitants of Jerusalem for sin and for uncleanness" (Zech. 13:1, KJV). That fountain is the precious blood of Jesus. The atonement He made for sinners by His death on the cross is the central theme of the gospel. It is the sun around which all other truths revolve. It is the very essence of the gospel, for if it is taken away, nothing of the gospel message will remain. It is the ground of our faith and the very basis of the sinner's hope.

Modernism and evolutionary theories seek to dam the stream of the precious blood of Jesus shed for sinners and thus rob Him of His divinity and power, for "without shedding of blood there is no remission" of sin (Heb. 9:22). It would be difficult to faithfully study the abounding evidence of the deity of Christ and His exalted greatness without concluding that His atonement has infinite value and efficacy.

If Jesus was a mere man or even an angel, His death would have had no salvific value to a lost world, for the death of a human or angel could never satisfy divine justice, appease divine law, effect pardon for our sins, ease the guilty conscience, or bring about redemption of the soul. It would have had no efficacy whatsoever; no purpose would have been served.

The atonement He made for sinners by His death on the cross is the central theme of the gospel. It is the sun around which all other truths revolve.

If the deity of Christ is successfully refuted, then the atonement is a failure, and all people are still lost in their sins. However, if His deity stands, then the atonement also stands, and by its effulgent glory, it dispels the shadows of the tomb. Adam and all his posterity broke God's moral law, and this law demands the death of the transgressor. If it could have been set aside, then sinners would have gone free, and Jesus would not need to die. However, this would have caused Satan to triumph and brought in a reign of anarchy, terror, and eternal night throughout God's entire creation.

The Lord created a perfect universe in which He intended harmony, peace, and love to reign. This was marred when, in his heart, Lucifer developed jealousy, pride, and rebellion. He is a created being like all the other angels are. He wanted to be included in the government of God, and this instilled in him pride and jealousy, which led to war in heaven (see Isa. 14:12–14; Ezek. 28:12–17; Rev. 12:7–9). As a result, he was cast out of the paradise of God, and planet earth was the only place where he was able to find an abode. He soon corrupted Adam and Eve into doubting and disobeying God. Because of this, they had to leave their home in the Garden of Eden, lest they and their offspring should eat of the tree of life and live forever as perpetual wrongdoers.

Look at the havoc in our world today—crimes perpetuated one against the other—and multiply that by the vast population of people who have lived in the past. You will then better understand the havoc that sin would have caused if eternally perpetuated, as well as why God sent His Son to remedy the situation. He will come again to redeem all those who have believed on His name from this sin-cursed world. Then He will make a new world, as it originally was intended, and rid it of all sin and rebellion.

There was only one way to save doomed humanity from everlasting damnation, and that was for God to become our surety, assume our guilt, and die in our stead. This He did not hesitate to do since from before the foundation of the world, He had a plan. The decretive will of God will never be defeated. He wants mankind to enjoy freedom, as do all the rest of His creation.

The essence of God's character is love. For pure, genuine love to flourish, there must be freedom. Love cannot be forced or coerced. Satan, on the other hand, governs by forcing the will of others. God could not, in unmitigated divinity, come to die and fulfill the demands of the law on humanity's behalf because He is immortal and can never die. To suffer and die in our place, He had to become human. This was God's plan before the foundation of the world was laid.

If the devil knew this, he would have tried to frustrate God's eternal plan for mankind's redemption. When Adam and Eve disobeyed Jehovah, He promised He would send a Redeemer (see Gen. 3:15). When the proper time came, He sent forth His Son to be humanity's Savior. The complexity of the process is an amazing tapestry of the deep love of God for us. It reveals the intricate movement in the history of redemption, so wonderful when revealed and understood that it is just amazing.

This is revealed in volumes written by holy men of God (approximately forty different writers) over a period of 1,500 years. These different penmen wrote as they were moved by the Holy Spirit. Quite frequently, these writers did not even understand what they were writing, mainly because it was not only for them and their time. "[God] gave His only begotten Son" as a ransom for the fallen race, "that whoever believes in Him should not perish but have everlasting life. For God did not send His Son into the world to condemn the world, but that the world through Him might be saved" (John 3:16, 17).

The prophets of old predicted the coming of Jesus Christ into the world centuries before it happened. Moses, Ezekiel, Isaiah, Jeremiah, Hosea, Daniel, the psalmists, and others all wrote as the Holy Spirit directed them. They usually did not communicate with each other. Some lived hundreds of years apart; others were within the same period, but unconnected; yet there is a harmony in the message that fits together so neatly, revealing the unity that only the unseen will of God could have ordained. Some prophets spoke of kings who would be used by the Lord to intervene in the deliverance of His people, identifying them by name.

One cannot help but be astounded by the remarkable power of God to direct in the affairs of people to bring about His purpose for the salvation of mankind. He revealed to the prophet Daniel the exact date when the Jews would return from their exile in Babylon, as well as the pagan king who would supply the means for the expense of the journey and the materials for the rebuilding of the temple in Jerusalem.

This is part of the longest time prophecy in the Word of God that includes the exact time of the Messiah's birth, baptism, and when He would be cut off, but not for Himself. This time prophecy has even extended down to our period in history.

> Though corruption and defiance might be seen in every part of the alien province, a way for its recovery was

provided. At the very crisis, when Satan seemed about to triumph, the Son of God came with the embassage of divine grace. Through every age, through every hour, the love of God had been exercised toward the fallen race. Notwithstanding the perversity of men, the signals of mercy had been continually exhibited. And when the fullness of time had come, the Deity was glorified by pouring upon the world a flood of healing grace that was never to be obstructed or withdrawn till the plan of salvation should be fulfilled.

Satan was exulting that he had succeeded in debasing the image of God in humanity. Then Jesus came to restore in man the image of his Maker. None but Christ can fashion anew the character that has been ruined by sin. He came to expel the demons that had controlled the will. He came to lift us up from the dust, to reshape the marred character after the pattern of His divine character, and to make it beautiful with His own glory. (White, *The Desire of Ages*, pp. 37, 38)

The whole territory was illuminated by the light from the angelic hosts of God as they announced the Savior's birth to shepherds keeping watch over their flocks by night on the plains of Bethlehem Ephratah. When the angels departed, the shepherds, still amazed, said one to another, "Let us now go to Bethlehem and see this thing that has come to pass" (Luke 2:15). They went and found the baby wrapped in swaddling clothes, lying in a manger because there was no room in the inn. The only place they could find was a cow stall where the animals stayed.

Seven hundred years before the Messiah's birth, the prophet Isaiah foretold it (see 7:14; 9:6, 7). Matthew recorded that, although Jesus Christ, who created all things, was expected, when He was born, His parents could find no comfortable place for Him to stay. When He grew into manhood, His disciples asked Him where He was staying. The Creator of the universe replied, "Foxes have holes and birds of the air *have* nests, but the Son of Man has nowhere to lay *His* head" (Matt. 8:20).

Everywhere the Savior of the world went, crowds followed Him. He performed miracles of healing, raised the dead to life again, restored sight to the blind, cleansed lepers, fed the hungry, calmed the angry, storm-tossed sea, cast demons out of possessed victims, and taught the people, everywhere He went, about the kingdom of heaven and love of God for all mankind.

Jesus came to this earth to die for the sins of every person who has ever lived. One would have expected that the leaders of the people would have welcomed Him with open arms. For centuries, they were taught that God would send them a Savior who would rescue His people from their sins. Each succeeding generation heard the same message, and each family passed on the same history of their escape from Egyptian slavery.

On God's instructions, Moses taught the people how to prepare for the Passover feast. They were instructed on how to carefully select the best lamb from the flock—a one-year-old male. It was to be free of any injury or disease. It was to be carefully selected on the tenth day of the first month and separated from the rest of the herd. Four days later, the lamb was to be killed and prepared. It was not to be boiled, but instead, roasted whole, and its bones were not to be broken. There was to be one lamb for each family. If there was a family who had no lamb, they were to share with a neighbor.

The Passover meal was to be prepared and eaten with bitter herbs. All members of the household were to be dressed and ready to travel. The father would paint the posts and lintel of the door of the house with the blood of the slain lamb (but not the floor). All members of the family would eat the Passover meal. This signified the Lamb of God who was to come to be slain for the remission of their sins. The Hebrew people were to keep this feast throughout all their generations in remembrance of their flight from Egyptian slavery.

This feast is still observed by Jewish families all over the world as a solemn memorial of their flight from Egypt. it points to Jesus the Lamb of

God who would come to give His life as a ransom for the sins of the whole world. God arranged that Jesus would fulfill all the prophecies concerning Him. He was arrested and subjected to unlawful trials (it was unlawful for the Sanhedrin to hold secret trials at night, which they did; and the high priest to tear his robe and slap the Son of God, which he did).

When they could produce no truthful witness, they contrived trumped-up accusations against Jesus. The Lamb of God was slain for our sins. He died the death we deserve so that we may have the life that is His, unborrowed. In the entire universe, there was no one qualified to die for our sins, except Christ, and this He did willingly. From His thirtieth birthday, He celebrated three Passovers, and on the fourth Passover, He gave His life as a ransom for many.

Jesus died according to the deliberate will of God the Father, who is by no means sadistic, but willing to do whatever necessary to redeem humanity. Before He was crucified, our Savior declared, "Therefore My Father loves Me, because I lay down My life that I may take it again. No one takes it from Me, but I lay it down of Myself. I have power to lay it down, and I have power to take it again. This command I have from My Father" (John 10:17, 18). Reading a little further:

> Then the Jews surrounded Him and said to Him, "How long do You keep us in doubt? If You are the Christ, tell us plainly." Jesus answered them, "I told you, and you do not believe. The works that I do in My Father's name, they bear witness of Me. But you do not believe, because you are not My sheep, as I said to you. My sheep hear My voice, and I know them, and they follow Me. And I give them eternal life, and they shall never perish; neither shall anyone snatch them out of My hand. My Father, who has given *them* to Me, is greater than all; and no one is able to snatch *them* out of My Father's hand. I and *My* Father are one." (John 10:24–30)

At the ninth hour (3 p.m.), the very time when the evening sacrifice was to be offered, Jesus, on Calvary's cross, declared, "It is finished!" At that instant, the knife fell from the hand of the priest, and the lamb for the evening sacrifice escaped. Simultaneously, the veil separating the Holy Place from the Most Holy Place was torn in two from the top to the bottom as the eternal Son of God gave His life for the sins of the world. His plan for the salvation of all mankind was now effected. The price for sin's ransom was fully paid by the precious blood of the Lamb.

The day of Christ's crucifixion was also the day before the Sabbath, the seventh and last day of the week. Jesus kept the Sabbath, even in death. On Sunday morning, before the break of day, the Son of God came forth from the tomb. He is indeed the Resurrection and the Life. Death could not bind Him, and the tomb could not stifle Him. His resurrection confirmed that God the Father had accepted His sacrifice for humanity.

When Satan took Jesus to the mountaintop and offered to give Him the kingdoms of this world with their earthly glory, he was thus offering Jesus the crown without the cross. It was a shortcut to securing the rulership of this world. Although Jesus is a friend of sinners and desires to offer them salvation, there would be no circumventing God's plan.

Jesus died according to the deliberate will of God the Father, who is by no means sadistic, but willing to do whatever necessary to redeem humanity.

For the earth to be restored to His kingdom and men and women to become His subjects, Christ first had to prepare the way for sinners to be transformed into living saints. This He could do only by going to the cross. Jesus is the Creator of all mankind, but He is also God of the righteous specifically. If sinners are to be freed from the sentence of eternal death, He must suffer that sentence for them, for "without shedding of blood there is no remission." There was no other way.

It was not an easy undertaking, but for our sakes "He endured the cross" to deliver sinners from sin and its penalty and finally restore them to their long-lost Edenic estate. Christ presented Himself a sacrifice for humanity's sins. No other conclusion can be deduced from the many statements of Scripture that declare that His death was made an atonement for sin. His sacrifice was so complete, and His priestly ministry so efficacious, that through these means the sins of His people may be entirely blotted out.

"But he was wounded for our transgression, he was bruised for our iniquities; the chastisement of our peace was upon him; and with his stripes we are healed. All we like sheep have gone astray; we have turned every one to his own way; and Jehovah hath laid on him the iniquity of us all" (Isa. 53:5, 6, ASV). Let us take note that His healing comes through His stripes. It was *our* transgressions and iniquities for which He suffered and died as a sinner, not His own.

"Him who knew no sin he made *to be* sin on our behalf, that we might be made the righteousness of God in him" (2 Cor. 5:21, ASV). "[I]n whom we have our redemption through his blood, the forgiveness of our trespasses, according to the riches of his grace" (Eph. 1:7, ASV). "[I]n whom we have our redemption, the forgiveness of our sins" (Col. 1:14, ASV). "[T]his is my blood of the covenant, which is poured out for many unto remission of sins" (Matt. 26:28, ASV).

Why was this divine sacrifice made? Why did the Son of God die as a sinner? He did it for us. Yes, He did it for you and me. Pilate declared, "I find no cause for death in Him." How true! The cause of death was in us. We were supposed to pay the wages of sin; we were under condemnation, and Jesus stepped in and took our place and punishment. His blood brought redemption to us.

That is what Christ did for every sinner. He tasted death for everyone. He was sinless, though He bore the burden of sin for us. Jesus became sin for us. He so closely identified Himself with sinners that He carried the entire load of guilt that we would otherwise bare. He suffered the same remorse and shame that unrepentant sinners will suffer after the door of mercy is finally closed, and they are required to answer for their lives of sin.

Christ took our place. It was not His sins that He carried, for He had no sin. Not one taint was found in Him. The sins that He bore were yours and mine. "Which of you convinceth me of sin?" He asked (John 8:46). Could anyone? He was the sinless, spotless Lamb of God. He was loaded down with the sins of the entire world. It was the sins of every man, every woman, every child that has ever lived that He carried on His body on that tree. It was man's sins that weighed Him down. So heavy was the load that Christ carried. "He temporarily lost the assurance that if He suffered death in man's behalf, He would come forth from the grave" (Branson 2002, p. 38).

The apostle Peter said of Christ, "Who committed no sin, Nor was deceit found in His mouth" (1 Peter 2:22; ref. Isa. 53:9). His chosen people rejected Him and freed a murderer instead. Pilate, the gutless, spineless Roman governor, succumbed to the veiled threats of the Jewish leaders and mob and crucified Jesus, who suffered the most heinous assault imaginable to save all who, by faith, will trust Him as Savior and Lord.

If we were there, would we have done otherwise? It is doubtful that we would have, for keep in mind that it was our sins that sent Him to shed His blood on that cruel cross. Isaiah wrote, "All we like sheep have gone astray; We have turned, every one, to his own way; And the LORD has laid on Him the iniquity of us all" (53:6). Your sins and mine sent the Son of God to die. If we should fail to yield complete allegiance to Him, there will be no salvation; only a fearful looking forward to the judgment seat of Almighty God!

CHAPTER 7

Signs of Our Times

Everywhere one turns today, one sees radical changes taking place in rapid succession, at an alarming rate, that demonstrate maddening, pell-mell, staccato patterns. Some of these changes are positive, while many are questionable at best, depending on perspective. One thing is definite, however: it is that most, if not all, of these occurrences are fulfillments of Bible prophecy.

For instance, in the fifth century BC, the God of heaven gave His prophet Daniel, a captive living in Babylon during the reign of Nebuchadnezzar, visions of things that were to take place during his lifetime, in the centuries that would succeed this monarchy, and all the way down to the days in which we are now living—the end of time. At the time when Daniel received his visions, people (the Babylonians, anyway) perhaps thought life was good. They thought they were progressive, and from the record of what the king thought at the time, life was very good, causing his haughty outburst, which had severe consequences for him, if no one else. It has been said that pride goes before a fall.

> "Is not this great Babylon, that I have built for a royal dwelling by my mighty power and for the honor of my majesty?" While the word *was still* in the king's mouth, a voice fell from heaven: "King Nebuchadnezzar, to you it is spoken: the kingdom has departed from you! And they shall drive you from men, and your dwelling *shall be* with the beasts of the field. They shall make you eat grass like oxen; and seven times shall pass over you, until you know that the Most High rules in the kingdom of men, and gives it to

whomever He chooses." That very hour the word was fulfilled concerning Nebuchadnezzar; he was driven from men and ate grass like oxen; his body was wet with the dew of heaven till his hair had grown like eagles' *feathers* and his nails like birds' *claws*. (Daniel 4:30–33)

Many people have said that history tends to repeat itself. All too frequently, when the Almighty God of heaven smiles on mere mortals and entrusts them with the power to rule in the affairs of His people, they soon forget that they are only dust and start lording it over their "subjects." Not long afterward, they begin crushing the life out of their fellow citizens while pretending to have their best interests at heart. They forget that God sees everything and does not sleep. At such times, He may very well choose to teach valuable lessons in humility, with lasting, positive effects.

All that aside, the rapidity with which changes are occurring in the twenty-first century seems apt to alert each of us to the fact that the King of kings and Lord of lords is knocking at the door.

All that aside, the rapidity with which changes are occurring in the twenty-first century seems apt to alert each of us to the fact that the King of kings and Lord of lords is knocking at the door.

It is a reminder to all of us that we need to set our lives and houses in order and be ready to greet Him when He comes. I hope you, dear reader, will agree. Either way, I need to follow my own counsel and set my house in order so that I can meet and greet the returning Savior. By His grace and mercy, I hope to see you at the Father's house. Who knows, perhaps with the way this world is dissolving, it could be sooner than anyone thinks.

Peace and grace be with you all. God is gracious, loving, merciful, and kind. He allows the sun to shine upon the godly and ungodly alike. He is an equal opportunity employer. He is love. Again, I must take my own advice and get ready to meet Him when He comes, which I really hope will be very soon. I am writing these things as your brother in Christ.

Oh, by the way, I was hoping to avoid stepping on anyone's toes, but I cannot avoid this issue, though I will avoid specifying names. God has ordained that governments are to be for the orderly rule of the people. However, when leaders in the upper echelon claim that their primary reason for being in positions of leadership is to drain the swamp, only to discover that when they take a solemn oath to rule, they have flooded the swamp instead, which only makes things worse.

That was obvious all along. Before they were elected, it was clear, by the language, lifestyle, and refusal to do what every other person who sought to become president has been willing to do—release past income tax statements—where this administration was headed. There is only one reason why a candidate would refuse to comply. That was quite obvious before. When Nixon was declaring that he was not a crook, I remember one loyal citizen stating, "If you walk like a duck, and you quack like a duck, you must be a duck!"

About what am I rambling? I am sure that that power-hungry lot at the top who embraced this "fine gentleman" knew all along what they were getting. They could have prevented the swamp in which they now find themselves if they were honest. I suppose one would think that they would have if they could have. Then again, "What a tangled web we weave, when first we practice to deceive."

I know I may have stirred the pot, but I sensed the need to speak the truth, or at least give my honest assessment. From the events we see happening around us, the Righteous Judge is at the door! Ready or not, He is coming soon. To those who insist on harboring sin, I must ask, "Are you ready? Where are you planning to hide when that great day comes?" It may seem like I'm pointing a finger, but I have three fingers pointing back at me. I hope you know the Judge. If you do, you will have nothing to fear.

CHAPTER 8

The Wonderful Condescension of Christ

Inasmuch then as the children have partaken of flesh and blood, He Himself likewise shared in the same, that through death He might destroy him who had the power of death, that is, the devil, and release those who through fear of death were all their lifetime subject to bondage. For indeed He does not give aid to angels, but He does

> give aid to the seed of Abraham. Therefore, in all things He had to be made like *His* brethren, that He might be a merciful and faithful High Priest in things *pertaining* to God, to make propitiation for the sins of the people. For in that He Himself has suffered, being tempted, He is able to aid those who are tempted. (Hebrews 2:14–18)

If the devil could have caused Jesus to yield even once, the entire human race would have been lost, for then He could not have been the representative of the race. This is the wonderful condescension of Christ and the divine mystery of the eternal ages. The doctrine of the incarnation of Christ in human flesh is a mystery, "Even the mystery which hath been hid from ages and from generations…" (Col. 1:26, KJV). It is the great, profound mystery of godliness. Scripture tells us, "And the Word was made flesh, and dwelt among us" (John 1:14, KJV). Christ took upon Himself human nature, a nature far inferior to His heavenly, divine nature. Nothing shows the wonderful condescension of God like this does.

Jesus did not pretend to assume human nature. "He was the Son of Mary; He was of the seed of David according to human descent. He is declared to be a man, even the Man Christ Jesus. 'This Man,' writes Paul, 'was counted worthy of more glory than Moses, inasmuch as He who hath builded the house hath more honor than the house'" (White 1988, p. 74). "For *there is* one God and one Mediator between God and men, *the* Man Christ Jesus" (1 Tim. 2:5).

> God, who at sundry times and in divers manners spake in time past unto the fathers by the prophets, Hath in these last days spoken unto us by *his* Son, whom he hath appointed heir of all things, by whom also he made the worlds; Who being the brightness of *his* glory, and the express image of his person, and upholding all things by the word of His power, when He had by himself purged

our sins, sat down on the right hand of the Majesty on high. (Hebrews 1:1–3, KJV)

Therefore, just as through one man sin entered the world, and death through sin, and thus death spread to all men, because all sinned… so also by one Man's obedience many will be made righteous. (Romans 5:12–19)

Jesus was the Commander of heaven, equal with the Father, yet He condescended to lay aside His crown and royal robe and clothed His divinity with humanity to save our race. The incarnation of Christ in human flesh is a mystery. He could have come to earth as One with a remarkable appearance, unlike the children of mankind. His countenance could have shone with glory; His form could have been remarkable. Jesus could have presented an appearance that would charm any who would behold Him. However, this was not according to the plan devised in the courts of God. He was to bear the characteristics of the human family through the Jewish race.

> *Jesus was the Commander of heaven, equal with the Father, yet He condescended to lay aside His crown and royal robe and clothed His divinity with humanity to save our race.*

In all respects, the Son of God was to wear the same features as did other human beings. He was not to have such beauty as would make Him singular among others. He was to attract no attention to Himself. He came as a representative of the human family. He was to stand as mankind's substitute and surety. He was to live as we do in such a way as to contradict Satan's assertion that humanity was his everlasting possession and God Himself could not take it out of his hands.

If Christ had come in His divine form, humanity could not have endured the sight. The contrast would have been too painful, and the glory too overwhelming. People could not have survived the presence of One so pure, bright, and glorious. Therefore, He did not assume His divine nature or even that of angels. He came in the likeness of mankind and took upon Himself our nature. He is and henceforth shall ever be both fully God and fully clothed in humanity. He was sinless and thus able to be our Savior.

"But thirty years was all that the world could endure of Immanuel. For thirty years He dwelt in a world all seared and marred with sin, doing the work that no other one ever had done or ever could do" (White 1956, p. 1131). Christ Jesus fulfilled that which was prophesied: "He Himself took our infirmities And bore *our* sicknesses" (Matt. 8:17; ref. Isa. 53:4).

"For we do not have a High Priest who cannot sympathize with our weaknesses, but was in all *points* tempted as *we are,* yet without sin" (Hebrews 4:15). In taking upon Himself human nature in its fallen condition, Christ did not in the least participate in its sin. He was subject to the infirmities and weaknesses by which humanity is surrounded, thereby fulfilling Isaiah's prophecy.

> "In Him was life; and the life was the light of men." It is not physical life that is here specified, but eternal life, the life which is exclusively the property of God. The Word, who was with God, and who was God, had this life. Physical life is something which each individual received. It is not eternal or immortal; for God, the Lifegiver, takes it again. Man has no control over his life. But the life of Christ was unborrowed. No one can take this life from Him. "I lay it down of myself," He said. In Him was life, original, unborrowed, underived. This life is not inherent in man. He can possess it only through Christ. He cannot earn it; it is given him as a free gift if he will believe in Christ as his personal Saviour. "This is life eternal, that they might know thee the only true God, and Jesus Christ, whom thou hast sent." John 17:3. This is the open fountain of life for the world....

> ...How wide is the contrast between the divinity of Christ and the helpless infant in Bethlehem's manger... Far higher than any of the angels, equal with the Father in dignity and glory, and yet wearing the garb of humanity! Divinity and humanity were mysteriously combined, and man and God became one. It is in this union that we find the hope of our fallen race. Looking upon Christ in humanity, we look upon God, and see in Him the brightness of His glory, the express image of His person...
>
> ...Christ did not make-believe take human nature; He did verily take it. He did in reality possess human nature. "As the children are partakers of flesh and blood, he also himself likewise took part of the same." He was The Son of Mary; He was of the seed of David according to human descent. He is declared to be a man, even the man Christ Jesus. "This man," writes Paul, "was counted worthy of more glory than Moses, inasmuch as he who hath builded the house hath more honor than the house." (White, *The SDA Bible Commentary*, vol. 5, p. 1130)

Indeed, Christ, the second person of the Trinity, was the spotless, sinless Lamb of God, delivered up as a ransom for all those who believe and accept His free grace and mercy.

If Satan could have tempted Christ to sin, he would have bruised the Savior's head. As it was, he could only touch the Redeemer's heel. If he could have caused Jesus to yield even once, the hope of the human race would have perished. Divine wrath would have come upon Christ as it came upon Adam. He and the church would have been without hope.

We should have no misgivings regarding the perfect sinlessness of the human nature of Christ. Our faith must be an intelligent faith, looking unto Him in perfect confidence and full, entire belief in the atoning sacrifice.

> As you therefore have received Christ Jesus the Lord, so walk in Him, rooted and built up In Him and established

in the faith, as you have been taught, abounding in it with thanksgiving. Beware lest anyone cheat you through philosophy and empty deceit, according to the tradition of men, according to the basic principles of the world, and not according to Christ. For in Him dwells all the fullness of the Godhead bodily; and you are complete in Him, who is the head of all principality and power. (Colossians 2:6–10)

"And without controversy great is the mystery of godliness: God was manifested in the flesh, Justified in the Spirit, Seen by angels. Preached among the Gentiles, Believed on in the world, Received up into glory" (1 Tim. 3:16). Jesus came to live in the likeness of mankind and made Himself of no reputation so that He could be a better representative of our race.

The Savior was above all prejudice toward nations or people. He was willing to extend the blessings and privileges of the Jews to all who would accept the light that He came to the world to bring. Jesus came into the world to reveal to humanity the love and mercy of God. He came to die for the sins of all mankind.

To all who accept God's forgiveness, the Savior of the world says, "Come unto Me, and I will give you rest from your burden and load of sin." To Christ has been committed all judgment because He is the Son of Man. Nothing escapes His knowledge. He is infinite in righteousness, goodness, and truth. He is mighty to withstand principalities, powers, and spiritual wickedness in high places. He came to redeem this world from the curse of sin and power of Satan.

When Christ came to earth, He saw how extensively and rampantly sin had corrupted the world. He planted the cross between earth and heaven, divinity and humanity. When the Father saw the cross, He was satisfied. "It is enough," He said. The offering for sin was complete. Jesus had paid it all. God and humanity can now be reconciled. "Mercy and truth have met together; Righteousness and peace have kissed" (Ps. 85:10). He promised that He would come again to reap from the earth all those who believe on His Word and place their trust in Him as Savior and Lord (see John 14:1–3). He keeps His word. His promises are sure.

Jesus wants all who have trusted Him as Savior and Lord of their lives to remain watchful and ready to meet Him when He comes. We do not know when He will return, but He told us of things that would occur as His advent draws closer (see Matt. 24, 25). Each day brings us nearer to the day when our Redeemer will appear. As you are watching for His coming, be careful. Watch out for imposters—false christs and prophets. Jesus is coming soon. Be ready to greet Him. Do not allow anyone to steal your crown. Faithfully walk each day and trust in God.

CHAPTER 9

Jesus Will Come Again

"So Christ was once offered to bear the sins of many; and unto them that look for him shall he appear the second time without sin unto salvation" (Heb. 9:28, KJV). When Jesus was crucified on Calvary's cross, His act of giving His life made possible the redemption of humanity from sin and its influence and control. At that moment, mankind's rescue was not completed, though the price had been paid. After His resurrection, Christ ascended to heaven, leaving His followers behind in a world cursed with sin and its ravages. Most of the saints of past ages were still sleeping in their graves. He had announced to His disciples, "I go to My Father" (John 14:12). To Simon Peter, He said, "Where I am going you cannot follow Me now, but you shall follow Me afterward" (13:36).

As long as Christian men and women are surrounded by sin and subject to its influences; as long as the grave holds Jesus' sleeping followers; as long as the curse of lawlessness continues upon the earth, the plan of redemption not be complete. God's plan for the salvation of humanity involves more than the forgiveness of sin and victory over its effect. It includes the restoration of humanity's Edenic home, resurrection of the body, bestowal of immortality, and complete destruction of Satan, sin, and unrepentant sinners.

God has promised, "Affliction will not rise up a second time" (Nah. 1:9). The apostle Paul stated, "[W]e ourselves groan within ourselves, eagerly waiting for the adoption, the redemption of our body" (Rom. 8:23). Christ is the head of the church and the Savior of the body (see Eph. 5:23). "And the God of peace will crush Satan under your feet shortly" (Rom. 16:20).

As long as Christian men and women are surrounded by sin and subject to its influences; as long as the grave holds Jesus' sleeping followers; as long as the curse of lawlessness continues upon the earth, the plan of redemption not be complete.

These things were not accomplished at the time of Christ's first coming. His death and resurrection made their realization possible, but not an accomplished fact yet. The bodies of the dead saints are still in their graves, and Satan continues to go about as a roaring lion seeking whom he may devour. The earth is still filled with increasing violence and in the hands of the wicked. The plan of redemption is, therefore, not yet completed, and were Jesus to remain absent from the world, its provisions would not reach completion. However, have no doubt, for Jesus is coming again! Oh, glorious truth!

This is the marvelous promise of the ages. Again note Jesus' parting message to His disciples, so feelingly spoken just before He separated from them and ascended to heaven: "Let not your heart be troubled; you believe in God, believe also in Me. In My Father's house are many mansions; if *it were* not *so*, I would have told you. I go to prepare a place for you. And if I go and prepare a place for you, I will come again and receive you unto Myself; that where I am, *there* you may be also" (John 14:1–3).

Yes, Jesus will come again. This is the sweetest message that ever entered human ears. He is coming "without sin unto salvation." He will not come this time as a sin-bearer, to suffer and die on mankind's behalf. He did that once and forever when He gave His life on Calvary's cross (see Rom. 6:9, 10; Heb. 7:27).

This time He will come to bring the fullness of salvation. He will come to finish His work. The return of Christ will be visual and literal. It will not be in secret. His ascension was a literal event, and so will be His second coming. When He went back to heaven, His disciples watched Him as He ascended until a cloud enveloped Him and received Him out of their sight. Angels from heaven, who appeared to the sorrowing followers, declared that He would return in the same manner as they had seen Him depart (see Acts 1:9–11).

Everywhere in Scripture, testimony abounds that the return of Jesus will be literal and visible. "Behold, he cometh with clouds; and every eye shall see him, and they *also* which pierced him: and all kindreds of the earth shall wail because of him. Even so, Amen" (Rev. 1:7, KJV). "For as the lightning cometh out of the east, and shineth even unto the west; so shall also the coming of the Son of man be" (Matt. 24:27, KJV).

Those who are alive when Christ returns will not need to be told that He is coming. When He was here on earth, He said that the way to heaven is a straight way that leads to life eternal, and only few will find it. Many will not be ready to meet Jesus when He comes the second time. He cautioned His followers and people everywhere, "Then the sign of the Son of Man will appear in heaven, and then all the tribes of the earth will mourn, and they will see the Son of Man coming on the clouds of heaven with power and great glory. And He will send His angels with a great sound of a trumpet, and they will gather together His elect from the four winds, from one end of heaven to the other" (24:30, 31).

> Then the sky receded as a scroll when it is rolled up, and every mountain and island was moved out of its place. And the kings of the earth, the great men, the rich men, the commanders, the mighty men, every slave and every free man, hid themselves in the caves and in the rocks of the mountains, and said to the mountains and rocks, "Fall on us and hide us from the face of Him who sits on the throne and from the wrath of the Lamb! For the great day of His wrath has come, and who is able to stand?" (Revelation 6:14–17)

That will be a tragic spectacle for those who are not prepared when Jesus comes to earth the second time. The sad part is that no one needs to be lost. In reality, it is far easier to be saved than it is to be lost. He came the first time to die and redeem as many as will turn from sin and trust Him as Savior and Lord. The next time, He will come as Judge of all the earth.

"For God so loved the world that He gave His only begotten Son, that whoever believes in Him [that means anyone who comes to Jesus in full repentance of sin] should not perish but have everlasting life" (John 3:16). God will save anyone who, by faith in His Son, comes to Him. He will not turn anyone away. Indeed, Jesus is coming again, and every eye will see Him. This time He comes as King of kings and Lord of lords. Each must choose to follow Him now, for when He appears, it will be too late. "Behold, now *is* the accepted time; behold, now *is* the day of salvation" (2 Cor. 6:2).

> For God did not send His Son into the world to condemn the world, but that the world through Him might be saved. He who believes in Him is not condemned; but he who does not believe is condemned already, because he has not believed in the name of the only begotten Son of God. And this is the condemnation, that the light has come into the world, and men loved darkness rather than light, because their deeds were evil. (John 3:17–19)

It is inexplicable that it is easy for everyone to be saved by Jesus our Creator, Redeemer, and coming King, yet stubborn pride leads many to refuse God's invitation to accept His free mercy and pardoning grace, which will give them entrance into heaven to be with God. They choose instead to suffer hell and be forever lost.

Friend, it is very easy to spend eternity with Jesus, but one must labor hard to be lost. "Amazing grace! How sweet the sound That saved a wretch like me! I once was lost, but now am found; Was blind, but now I see." Jesus' return will occur at a time when talk of wars and rumors of wars are rampant throughout the earth. Each time a peace treaty is signed, only a short time later it is broken. The Bible says, "For when they shall say, Peace and safety; then sudden destruction cometh upon them, as travail upon a woman with child; and they shall not escape" (1 Thess. 5:3, KJV).

The Word of God goes even further, for it reveals not only that there will be destruction rather than peace, but also details on how this will develop:

> Proclaim ye this among the Gentiles; Prepare war, wake up the mighty men, let all the men of war draw near; let

them come up: Beat your plowshares into swords, and your pruninghooks into spears: let the weak say, I *am* strong. Assemble yourselves, and come, all ye heathen, and gather yourselves together round about: thither cause thy mighty ones to come down, O LORD. Let the heathen be wakened, and come up to the valley of Jehoshaphat: for there will I sit to judge all the heathen round about. Put ye in the sickle, for the harvest is ripe: come, get you down; for the press is full, the fats overflow; for their wickedness *is* great. (Joel 3:9–13, KJV)

Here we have a paradox. The people say, "We will not learn war anymore; we will beat our swords into ploughshares." While talking peace, they were preparing for war. Today, America is still engaged in a sixteen-year war in Afghanistan. It's the longest war yet, with no end in sight. At the same time, there is ominous banter with North Korea. America is also threatening to tear up a peace treaty with Iran. It now rests with us to choose between life and death. God revealed to the prophet what the end would be:

And whereas thou sawest iron mixed with miry clay, they shall mingle themselves with the seed of men: but they shall not cleave one to another, even as iron is not mixed with clay. And in the days of these kings shall the God of heaven set up a kingdom, which shall never be destroyed: and the kingdom shall not be left to other people, *but* it shall break in pieces and consume all these [earthly] kingdoms, and it shall stand forever. Forasmuch as thou sawest that the stone was cut out of the mountain without hands, and that it brake in pieces the iron, the brass, the clay, the silver, and the gold; the great God hath made known to the king what shall come to pass hereafter: and the dream *is* certain, and the interpretation thereof sure. (Daniel 2:43–45, KJV)

"And this gospel of the kingdom shall be preached in all the world for a witness unto all nations; and then shall the end come" (Matt. 24:14, KJV). Friend, are you prepared to meet your God?

CHAPTER 10

Last Day Events

Matthew 24 is referred to as part of Jesus' Olivet Discourse. It is one of the final five discourses in this gospel account. It focuses on some details of God's coming judgment upon His opponents, as well as Christ's return. He commands His followers to be ever ready for His second advent, which is a strong motivation to remain faithful and obedient to His Word. In Matthew 23:37–39, we find the enemies of Jesus still plaguing Him. He came to His own, but His own did not receive Him. Therefore, on what turned out to be His final visit to the temple, He sorrowfully leaves it.

He left all the glories of heaven to come to this earth and give His life to redeem all humanity. Scripture says, "He came to His own, and His own did not receive Him. But as many as received Him, to them He gave the right to become children of God, to those who believe in His name: who were born, not of blood, nor of the will of the flesh, nor of the will of man, but of God" (John 1:11–13).

As Jesus looked over Jerusalem from the Mount of Olives, He was filled with deep sadness and declared, "See! Your house is left to you desolate" (Matt. 23:38). Soon after uttering these words, He departed forever from the precincts of the temple as He declared, "you shall see Me no more till you say, 'Blessed *is* He who comes in the name of the Lord'" (v. 39). That is a very tragic declaration, not for the Son of God, but especially for those who refused His offer of salvation. On that day, when they will have to give account at the judgment seat of Christ, they will have no savior or advocate to speak in their defense.

The question, therefore, is, How will they stand in the judgment on that great resurrection day? That is a question that all people will have to ask themselves if they refuse God's free salvation offered through the merits of Jesus Christ His Son. Today, as His return draws closer to fulfillment, just as in the days before the flood, there are skeptics and scoffers who still refuse to seek and submit to the Savior.

I began working on this manuscript in 2015, and now in 2019, even many of the people who deny the existence of God the Creator and profess not to care are concerned about the changes happening throughout the earth. Even the Roman Pontiff has commented that it appears that "World War III" is starting in many different areas of the world. Many other signs are occurring here in America and across the globe.

The purpose of all Bible prophecy, such as Matthew 24, is to motivate us to live well and walk in the footsteps of Jesus by faith in Him each day. It is not given to satisfy our curiosity about the future, but intensify our zeal and piety in the present. There is no mistaking Jesus' primary challenge to all believers: Be ready at all times. Do not let down your guard. Keep doing the work of the kingdom and preaching the gospel throughout the world. Do not become obsessed with the future, but invest yourself in the present so that you be prepared when the future arrives and you stand before the King of kings.

There are radical changes occurring in our world that cause many people to be perplexed and confused. Many are asking what these things mean. God's inspired Word provides the answer. One of the chief themes of the Bible is the return of Jesus Christ. It is mentioned 250 times in the New Testament alone. He predicted, while speaking to His disciples, the destruction of the beautiful temple: "Do you not see all these things? Assuredly, I say to you, not *one* stone shall be left here upon another, that shall not be thrown down" (Matt. 24:2).

The disciples were surprised and full of questions. "Tell us, when will these things be? And what *will* be the sign of Your coming, and of the end of the age" (v. 3)? In answering them, Jesus warned against deception by imposters claiming to be Him. Almost in the same breath, He also told of wars and rumors of wars, as the nations of earth rise against each other in conflict. He foretold famines, earthquakes in various places, and pestilences, tying all these troubles together as the beginning of sorrows (vs. 4–8).

> *The purpose of all Bible prophecy, such as Matthew 24, is to motivate us to live well and walk in the footsteps of Jesus by faith in Him each day. It is not given to satisfy our curiosity about the future, but intensify our zeal and piety in the present.*

In a masterful presentation, Jesus blended the two events. He discussed the signs that would precede the destruction of Jerusalem and events signaling occurrences at the end of the age. He used the disciples' question as a jumping-off point for a magnificent sermon about the signs foreshadowing His return. In Matthew 24 and 25, He predicted details of the coming judgment. These details clarify God's judgment on His opponents and prepare His followers for the time of the end of the age.

These chapters form a single unit but fall into two distinct portions: prophecy and preparation. In Matthew 24:1–41, Jesus highlights predictions about His return and the coming judgment. Then there is a turning point in verse 42. From here, He highlights preparations for His followers to be ready when the judgment comes. The first part of the discourse consists mainly of factual details about the future. The second part consists of commands showing believers how to live in preparation for future judgment. It is important to note that Matthew thematically linked the Olivet Discourse with the preceding series of conflicts (see 21:23–23:39).

The destruction of the temple occurred in AD 70, approximately forty years after Jesus returned to heaven, when the Romans laid siege against Jerusalem. Many of those who heard Him predict this event were most likely still alive and witnessed the fulfillment of this prophecy. When the Romans demolished the city, the first part of the Olivet Discourse was fulfilled.

Today, in the year 2019, the signs that Jesus predicted, which point to His second coming, are being fulfilled all around us. Matthew 24 contains more than twenty signs pointing to the Lord's return and the end of the age. Verse 6 relates to Revelation 11:18: "The nations were angry, and Your wrath has come, And the time… that You… should destroy those that destroy the earth."

In 1945, after the atomic bomb was dropped on Hiroshima, William Ripley stated, "I am standing today where the end of the world began. With nuclear weapons humanity now have the capacity for self-destruction." This is one of the signs of the nearness of Jesus' return. Today, more nations have acquired thermonuclear weapons of mass-destruction, and many are still threatening warfare upon other nations.

Where once there appeared to be more thoughtfulness and a desire to use diplomacy to settle differences, that no longer seems to be the case. Where once nations, although armed, were more willing to negotiate, now, in 2019, there is less willingness to resort to amicable channels. It's not a guarantee that one can retire to bed and wake up to an environment of peace and safety.

Today, there is an increase in the number of mass killings and the taking of human life. No one is safe any longer, for even in public schools there is no longer an assurance of children returning home safely from schools. We are living in a time that the Bible predicted, "when they say 'Peace and safety!' then sudden destruction comes upon them, as labor pains upon a pregnant woman. And they shall not escape" (1 Thess. 5:3).

"And there will be famines, pestilences, and earthquakes in various places" (Matt. 24:7). America was once called the breadbasket of the world, for she had what seemed to be an inexhaustible supply of grain and food to feed the nations of the world. Now it is estimated that more than 3.5 million people die of starvation each day worldwide, and that number is increasing.

It seems like yesterday when it appeared to be a rare occurrence to hear of someone taking another person's life. Today, it is unusual *not* to hear of mass-murders happening in all areas of the world. It is no longer safe for children to even attend schools, whether public or private. The value of human life is no longer given much consideration. As I am writing this book, just yesterday a gunman shooting from his hotel rooms wounded over five hundred people, and as of this moment, fifty-nine people from this incident were killed. Also, more nations are seeking nuclear armaments.

The reason for this wanton murder spree is still unknown. At the same time, nations are angry, while it seems there is no solution to the mounting chaos all over the land. As we get nearer to the return of Jesus, all this chaotic turmoil is prophesied to increase. As one looks around, it is evident that these prophecies from Matthew 24 are being fulfilled. Earthquakes, tornadoes, and hurricanes are far more severe and frequent than ever before, and this is enough to cause people who previously showed no interest in God, the Bible, or theology to ask questions as they notice the changes in the times and seasons.

There should be no doubt that the return of our Lord and Savior Jesus Christ is drawing nearer. More often we hear about many people expressing great fear of what the future holds. There will be a moral breakdown in society and an increase in crime. "And because iniquity shall abound, the love of many shall wax cold" (v. 12; see also 2 Tim. 3:1–4). Our heavenly Father has promised to keep His children in the time of trouble.

There will be a more prevalent conflict between capital and labor as we see the return of Jesus drawing closer. Conflict of this kind has always existed. However, since 2006, there has been greater restlessness and discontent as the economy has slowed down and wages have often become uncertain.

> Come now, *you* rich, weep and howl for your miseries that are coming upon *you*! Your riches are corrupted, and your garments are moth-eaten. Your gold and silver are corroded, and their corrosion will be a witness against you and will eat your flesh like fire. You have heaped up treasure in the last days. Indeed the wages of the laborers who mowed your fields, which you kept back by fraud, cry out; and the cries of the reapers have reached the ears of the ears of the Lord of Sabaoth. You have lived on the earth in pleasure and luxury; you have fattened your hearts as in the day of slaughter. You have condemned, you have murdered the just; he does not resist you. (James 5:1–6)

The Bible predicts a great desire for pleasure as people worship the goddess of hedonism. Jesus will raise up a people committed to the proclamation of the gospel of the kingdom, which segues us to Matthew 24:14, the most crucial sign of the end-time: "And this gospel of the kingdom will be preached in all the world as a witness to all the nations, and then the end will come." When we see these things happening, what should we do? "Watch therefore, and pray always that you may be counted worthy to escape all these things that shall come to pass, and to stand before the

Son of Man… lest your hearts be weighed down with… cares of this life, and that Day come on you unexpectedly" (Luke 21:36, 34).

These signs have, in one way or another, occurred from time to time, but when we see them happening more frequently and severely, take heed. For instance, the frequency with which we see wanton mass murders, senseless and unprovoked attacks by strangers, and the enormity of crimes committed without any concern for human life is unprecedented. The increasing rate of vicious murders committed by children, women, and the elderly should give us pause.

Today, it is perhaps safer to avoid a confrontation than stand one's ground. Jesus warned that when these signs occur, we as Christians are to pray often, hold fast to our faith, and look up, for our redemption draws nigh. In the physical world, there will be earthquakes, calamities, disasters, and signs in the sun, moon, and stars (see Luke 21:11; Matt. 24:29). In the business world, fear, distress, and perplexity exist on every side (see Luke 21:25, 26). Nations are in full preparation for war (see Joel 3:9, 10). Peace unions between nations will be enacted, then easily broken with the constant threat of war.

> *Today, it is perhaps safer to avoid a confrontation than stand one's ground. Jesus warned that when these signs occur, we as Christians are to pray often, hold fast to our faith, and look up, for our redemption draws nigh.*

All over the world, with trouble, uprisings, and threats of war, there is increasing pressure for religious legislation (see Rev. 13:12–17; 2 Tim.3:1–5). In the social world, there is a breakdown of morality (see Hosea 4:1–3), craze for fun and pleasure (see 2 Tim. 3:1–4), laxity in marriage (see Matt. 24:17), and rise in the tide of immorality (see Luke 17:28–30). There is also widespread scoffing against the gospel of the coming of Christ (see 2 Peter 3:3–5) and rebellion against the truth of God's Word (see 2 Tim. 4:3, 4; 1 Thess. 5:1–6).

Thankfully, the Lord has a counter to everything listed above: a worldwide movement of proclaiming the gospel of Christ's soon coming, effected through His remnant who keep His commandments (see Rev. 12:17; 14:6–14). Jesus says that when we see all these things, we will know that His coming is near, even at the door (see Matt. 24:33). "Therefore you also be ready, for the Son of Man is coming at an hour you do not expect" (24:44). Signs are also occurring more frequently in nature all over the world. Almost daily, one is sure to hear of some kind of calamity or disaster happening somewhere.

Here is something we ought to consider: For many years, there have been discussions on several fronts about climate change. However, noticeably absent from the discussions seems to be a biblical perspective. The discussion is about climatic conditions, yet it appears that no one has even thought to ask the Creator of these climatic conditions.

In August 2017, Hurricane Harvey devastated the entire city of Houston, Texas. Every home and business were affected. This is occurring as I write this book, while the threat of nuclear war is looming at the same time. There is a vast increase in activity in the scientific, manufacturing, and business worlds, while people's hearts are simultaneously failing them for fear of the things that are coming upon them.

Far more people are committing suicide, many of whom are seemingly far too young to even think about death, as well as the elderly. The concern of far too many is the uncertainty about what the future holds. Many can find no hope as they worry about what's in store for them. And yet, it is a good time to be alive as one surveys the situation and realizes the rapid advancement in knowledge and scientific developments, with which it is difficult to keep pace. This is a marvelous time to be young when there is so much to learn.

I sometimes try to go back in my mind to the prophet Daniel, when God gave him visions of the future age, and I realize that if he was alive to see these days in which we live, he would probably be amazed at the advancement in science. However, it is a sad period in history, for so many people seem to be losing all hope of coping with the changes and developments taking place. Nevertheless, it is also marvelous, even for those of advanced age, like the author of this book is.

Oh, come soon, Lord Jesus! What a loving and marvelous Creator to have designed all this from nothing! I can hardly wait to see the city that Jesus went to prepare. It is all so spectacular and grand!

CHAPTER 11

The Certainty of Christ's Return

All over our world, wherever the gospel of Jesus Christ, the Son of God, is preached, the His soon return is also proclaimed. World rulers realize that all their efforts at devising peace on earth are temporary at best. No matter what form of government mankind has devised, they have all failed, and peace treaties between nations are at best tenuous.

The Word of God gives a message of hope for humanity. When Jesus Christ was here on earth, He told His followers, before He went to the cross, that He was going back to His Father in heaven. They became very perplexed, and He told them that He was going to prepare a home for those who place their faith in Him and return to take them where He is: "Let not your heart be troubled; you believe in God, believe also in Me. In My Father's house are many mansions; if *it were* not so, I would have told you. I go to prepare a place for you. And if I go to prepare a place for you, I will come again and receive you to Myself; that where I am, *there* you may be also" (John 14:1–3).

Christians everywhere call this promise "the blessed hope." Christ's return is mentioned over 250 times in the New Testament alone. The prophets have spoken about this event over the centuries. For example, "Our God shall come, and shall not keep silent; A fire shall devour before Him, And it shall be very tempestuous all around Him" (Ps. 50:3). Also, "Now Enoch, the seventh from Adam, prophesied about these men also, saying: 'Behold, the Lord comes with ten thousands of His saints, to execute judgment on all, to convict all who are ungodly among them of all their deeds which they have committed in an ungodly way, and of all the harsh things which ungodly sinners have spoken against Him'" (Jude 14, 15).

After Christ resurrected from the dead, the disciples asked:

> "Lord, will You at this time restore the kingdom to Israel?" And He said to them, "It is not for you to know times or seasons which the Father has put in His own authority. But you shall receive power when the Holy Spirit has come upon you; and you shall be witnesses to Me in Jerusalem, and in all Judea and Samaria, and to the end of the earth." Now when He had spoken these things, while they watched, He was taken up, and a cloud received Him out of their sight. And while they looked steadfastly toward heaven as He went up, behold, two men stood by them in white apparel, who also said, "Men of Galilee, why do you stand gazing up into heaven? This *same* Jesus, who was taken up from you into heaven, will so come in like manner as you saw Him go up into heaven." (Acts 1:6–11)

Jesus' ascension to heaven was a real, literal event in history. He assures us that His return will also be a very real, literal, visible, and loud event. Every eye will see Him (see Rev. 1:7). He also warned us that false messiahs and prophets would arise and impersonate Him. He cautioned that many would claim that He is in the market place or some other location, but we should not believe it or see if the report is valid, because every eye will see Him when He comes, for His return will not be a secret or silent. "For as the lightning comes from the east and flashes to the west, so also will the coming of the Son of Man be" (Matt. 24:27). "For the Lord Himself will descend from heaven with a shout, with the voice of an archangel, and with the trumpet of God" (1 Thess. 4:16).

The main concern of Jesus' followers today, like every other age, is to believe the Bible. Nearly all His disciples were so sure of His return that they were willing to give their lives to prove the veracity of His promises. They all, in one way or another, paid a tremendous price in their defense of the gospel of Jesus. Many of them, under the influence of the Holy

Spirit, from their different perspectives, wrote the testimonies of their lives in Christ, which were in full harmony with the word of God revealed by the Old Testament prophecies, which were fulfilled in the New Testament.

Today, as in past centuries, there are still doubters and skeptics. The reason is that many are refusing to look at the evidence because if they did, they would then have no reason to doubt, and their excuses would vanish. The Word of God has stood the test of time. The evidence is irrefutably true. Through the centuries, men, women, and even children have stood firmly in defense of their faith in the gospel of Jesus Christ. Even today, Christians in many lands and various ways are taking a stand and paying dearly with their very lives.

After His cousin lost his head because he stood firmly for the Word of God, Jesus declared, "And from the days of John the Baptist until now the kingdom of heaven suffers violence, and the violent take it by force" (Matt. 11:12). The apostle Paul wrote of the blessedness of the gospel of Jesus Christ. "Therefore, since we have this ministry, as we have received mercy, we do not lose heart. But we have renounced the hidden things of shame, not walking in craftiness nor handling the word of God deceitfully, but by manifestation of the truth..." (2 Cor. 4:1, 2).

Yes, the gospel will go forward to the ends of the earth, telling people everywhere that Jesus, the eternal Son of God, came to earth and gave His life to save us from darkness, sin, hell, and all unrighteousness. Christ has commanded it, and it will be done before He returns. Paul declares that the ministry of the gospel has been given to us. The message in the Scriptures presents to us the reality that God is the Creator of the world and everything in it. We have, therefore, renounced the world and hidden things of shame, and this has caused a change in our lives as we allow the Holy Spirit to influence our hearts and minds.

In 2 Corinthians 4:3–4, the apostle draws our attention to the fact that in this world, a great controversy has been raging because Satan, the opposer of Jesus Christ, has rebelled against Him (see Isa. 14:12–18; Ezek. 28:12–15). He wants to keep the inhabitants of the earth in darkness about the mercies and goodness of God. As a result, many people have refused the knowledge of God's revelation (see Rom. 1). If we accept and believe the Word of God, then we should take it to heart and allow the Holy Spirit to transform our lives so that people all around us will see and believe the reality of the gospel, as they too come to understand what He has done to redeem us.

God is calling us to live out the mandate of the gospel of Jesus Christ (see 2 Cor. 4:5–7) and thereby awaken the awareness of people everywhere to His love and earnest desire to save them from the wrath that is coming upon the world. Paul reminds his readers that his message is not about himself or any other apostle; it is all about our Lord and Savior who has brought light into the world.

"For it is the God who commanded light to shine out of darkness, who has shone in our hearts to *give* the light of the knowledge of the glory of God in the face of Jesus Christ" (v. 6). Evangelists, past and present, have encountered major opposition to bring the light of the gospel to people everywhere. Many paid with their lives, and during the Dark Ages, the Word of God was hidden from the ordinary people, and the early reformers were persecuted, hunted down, and killed for proclaiming the gospel of Christ.

"*We are* hard-pressed on every side, yet not crushed [in spirit]; *we are* perplexed, but not in despair; persecuted, but not forsaken; struck down, but not destroyed (vs. 8, 9). Many of the early followers of Jesus suffered great hardship to bring the gospel to others. They faced death to bring

God's life-giving Word to those in darkness, and even today this difficult task continues. Paul draws our attention to the eternal world to come as he preaches the everlasting gospel. Satan, the enemy of our souls, is ever trying to make us despondent, but because of the Holy Spirit in our hearts and all that Christ suffered to save our souls, we are encouraged and do not need to lose heart.

"[D]o not look at the things which are seen, but at the things which are not seen. For the things which are seen *are* temporary, but the things which are not seen *are* eternal" (v. 18). We are to look through the eyes of faith to the time when Jesus will return to fulfill His promise and bring to a culmination the war between good and evil, which He already won on the cross of Calvary. His followers, in ages past, died believing with certainty in the blessed hope of His soon return. For whether we live or die, we are confident that Christ will come again someday. He has kept every promise that He has made, and each one was fulfilled on time.

CHAPTER 12

God's Final Message to Planet Earth

In the Book of Revelation, all the other books of the Bible meet their end, but none as much as Daniel does. Revelation is complementary to Daniel. In the latter, there are prophetic utterances for these last days. God told the aged seer, "But you, Daniel, shut up the words, and seal the book until the time of the end; many shall run to and fro, and knowledge shall increase" (12:4). We are now in the time of the end. A moment later, in response to his inquiry, the Lord said, "Many shall be purified, made white, and refined, but the wicked shall do wickedly; and none of the wicked shall understand…" (v. 10).

A wonderful feature of the prophetic word is that the people of God are never brought into positions of trials and difficulties and then abandoned. After taking them into scenes of tumult and danger, God carries them through to the end. He does not leave them there to guess their fate in doubt and despair (see Rev. 14:1–5).

A wonderful feature of the prophetic word is that the people of God are never brought into positions of trials and difficulties and then abandoned.

Revelation 13 closes with a view of the people of God—a small, weak, and defenseless company in deadly conflict with the mightiest powers of the earth, which the dragon is able to employ to his service. A decree is passed, backed up by the supreme power of the land, that they should worship the image and receive its mark under penalty of death if they refuse to comply. In the next scene, the apostle John beholds the same company standing on Mount Zion with the Lamb, victorious and playing on symphonic harps in the courts of heaven.

We are therefore assured that when the time of our conflict with the powers of darkness comes, deliverance is not only certain but guaranteed to the people of God. This is followed be His final messages of warning to planet earth. It is a call by three angelic messengers to those around the world. The first message is to be delivered "to every nation, tribe, tongue, and people—saying with a loud voice, 'Fear God and give glory to Him, for the hour of His judgment has come; and worship Him who made heaven and earth, the sea and springs of water" (14:6, 7).

The worship of God, the Creator of all things, is different from the worship of the beast and its image (see 13:8, 12, 15). In the soon-coming crisis, the inhabitants of earth will be called upon to make their choice, like the three Hebrew men were (see Dan. 3). The message of the first angel is designed to prepare all humanity to make the proper choice and stand firmly in the time of the final crisis. The Creator of the universe is the only being truly worthy of all worship. Worship is the prerogative of God alone, in contrast to all false gods.

The call to worship the God of heaven and earth as Creator of all things implies that due attention should be given to the sign of His creative work—the Sabbath (see Ex. 20:8–11; Isa. 58:13, 14). If people kept the Sabbath as God ordained, there would be more harmony among the nations. It would have served as a safeguard against infidelity, evolution, and the degradation of unity in society (see Acts 14:15; Rev. 13:16; White 1890, p. 336).

> And another angel followed, saying, "Babylon is fallen, is fallen, that great city, because she has made all nations drink of the wine of the wrath of her fornication." Then a third angel followed them, saying with a loud voice, "If anyone worships the beast and his image, and receives

his mark on his forehead or on his hand, he himself shall also drink of the wine of the wrath of God, which is poured out full strength into the cup of His indignation. He shall be tormented with fire and brimstone in the presence of the holy angels and in the presence of the Lamb. And the smoke of their torment ascends forever and ever; and they have no rest day or night, who worship the beast and his image, and whoever receives the mark of his name." Here is the patience of the saints; here *are* those who keep the commandments of God and the faith of Jesus. Then I heard a voice from heaven saying to me, "Write: 'Blessed *are* the dead who die in the Lord from now on.'" "Yes," says the Spirit, "that they may rest from their labors, and their works follow them." (Revelation 14:8–13)

We believe the 144,000 seen on Mount Zion are the saints who were, in Revelation 13, brought to view as objects of the wrath of the beast and his image. They are identical with those sealed in Revelation 7, who have already, as described, been shown to be the righteous ones who are alive at the second coming of Jesus Christ. They represent those who have been redeemed from among humanity (14:4); perhaps an example of living saints.

This Mount Zion is the same as the one from which the Lord projects His voice and speaks to His people in connection with the coming of the Son of Man (see Joel 3:16; Heb. 12:25–28; Rev. 16:17). Acceptance of the fact that there is a Mount Zion and New Jerusalem in heaven would be a powerful antidote for the false doctrine of a second probation and millennium of peace on earth. Another particular regarding the 144,000, in addition to those given in Revelation 7, will grab our attention: They have the name of the Lamb's Father written in their foreheads.

In Revelation 7, they are said to have the seal of God in their foreheads. An essential key to understanding this seal is thus furnished, for we at once perceive that the Father regards His name as His seal. The commandment that contains God's name is, therefore, the seal of the law. The Sabbath commandment is the only one that includes the descriptive title that distinguishes the true God from all false gods. Wherever this was placed, there the Father's name is said to be (see Deut. 12:5, 14, 18, 21; 14:23; 16:2, 6).

Therefore, whoever genuinely keeps the Sabbath has the seal of the living God. They sing a new song that no other company can learn. In Revelation 15:3, it is called the song of Moses and the song of the Lamb. The song of Moses (see Ex. 15) was a song of experience and deliverance. Thus, the song of the 144,000 is also a song of deliverance. No other can join in it, for no other group will have had an experience like theirs.

"[They] were not defiled with women" (Rev. 14:4). A woman in Bible prophecy symbolizes a church. A virtuous woman represents a pure church; a corrupt woman represents a false or apostate church. It is therefore characteristic of this company that at the time of their deliverance, they are not defiled by the fallen churches of the land or connected with them. However, we are not to conclude that they *never* had any connection with these churches, for it is only at a specific time that people become defiled by them.

In Revelation 18:4, we find a call issued to the people of God, while they are in Babylon, to come out, lest they become partakers of her sins. Heeding that call and leaving her association, they escape the defilement of her sins. Though some of the 144,000 may have once had a tie with corrupt, false churches, they sever that tie when it would become a sin to maintain it longer. "[They] follow the Lamb whithersoever He goeth" (14:4, KJV). We understand that this is spoken of them in their redeemed state. They are the special companions of their glorified Lord in the kingdom.

Of the same company and time, we read, "[T]he Lamb which is in the midst of the throne shall feed them, and shall lead them unto living fountains of waters" (Rev. 7:17, KJV). They are "firstfruits unto God and to the Lamb" (14:4). The different applications of this term denote special conditions. Christ is the first fruits as the antitype of the wave sheaf (see 1 Cor. 15:20, 23). The first receivers of the gospel are called a kind of first fruits (see James 1:18).

Therefore, the 144,000, being prepared for the heavenly gathering here on earth during the troublesome scenes of the last days, then translated to heaven without seeing death and occupying a preeminent position, are in this scene called first fruits unto God and the Lamb. With this triumphant description, the line of prophecy that began in Revelation 12 comes to a close.

> Then I saw another angel fly in the midst of heaven, having the everlasting gospel to preach to those who dwell on the earth—to every nation, tribe, tongue, and people—saying with a loud voice, "Fear God and give glory to Him, for the hour of His judgment has come; and worship Him who made heaven and earth, the sea and the springs of water. (Revelation 14:6, 7)

Another scene and chain of prophetic events are introduced in these verses. We know this to be so because the preceding verses describe a company of the redeemed in their immortal state, and this scene constitutes the close of the prophetic chain beginning in Revelation 12:1. Whenever we are brought through a line of prophecy to the end of the world, we know that that line ends there and what is subsequently introduced belongs to a new series of events.

The book of Revelation, in particular, is composed of these independent prophetic chains, as has already been outlined in many examples. The message described in these two verses is the first of what are known as "the three angels' messages." These angels are symbolic, for the work assigned them is that of preaching the everlasting gospel to the people. However, the preaching of the gospel has not been entrusted to literal angels but committed to men and women who are responsible for this sacred trust placed in their hands. Each of these three angels, therefore, symbolizes those who are commissioned to make known to their fellow brothers and sisters the distinct truths that constitute the burden of these messages.

Literal angels are intensely interested in the work of grace among mankind and sent forth by God to minister to those who shall be heirs of salvation. As there is order in all the movements and appointments of the Lord's domain, it may not be fanciful to suppose that a literal angel has charge and oversight of the work of each message (see Heb. 1:14; Rev. 1:1, 22:16). In these symbols, we see the sharp contrast the Bible draws between earthly and heavenly things.

Whenever earthly governments are represented, even the best of them, the most appropriate symbol that one finds is a wild beast. However, when the work of God is represented, an angel, clad in beauty and girded with power, is the chosen symbol. The importance of the work outlined in Revelation 14:6–12 will be apparent to anyone who studies it.

One should not assume that humanity will devote significant attention to the three angels' messages *en masse,* for in any period of this earth's history, the present truth for that time has too often been ignored by the majority. However, these messages constitute the theme to which the people will be most attentive if they are awake to what concerns their highest interests. When God commissions His ministers to announce to the world that the hour of His judgment has come, Babylon has fallen, and whoever worships the beast and his image must drink of His wrath, poured out full-strength into the cup of His indignation—a threat far more terrible than any other found in the Scriptures—no one, except at the peril of his or her soul, can treat these warnings as nonessential or with neglect.

This is especially true today when so much evidence testifies to the soon coming of earth's close. The angel of Revelation 14:6 is called "another angel" because John previously saw an angel similarly flying in the midst of heaven (see 8:13), proclaiming that the last three of the seven trumpets are woes. The first point to be determined is when this message is to be proclaimed. The text says, "the hour of His judgment has come" (14:7). This leaves little doubt that the proclamation is to be immediate—in our day—and we will discover more positive proof as we proceed.

This should set every pulse racing and heart beating madly. We find no record that, in the past, a proclamation went forth that the hour of God's judgment came in the days of the early church. From that apostolic period, nothing took place that could be construed as having such urgency. If that had occurred, it would have been untrue.

Revelation 14:6–11 is supposed to relate to the period of the Reformation, according to some Bible interpreters. However, there seems to be insuperable objections to these interpretations. Neither could it be said in consistency with truth, at the time of the Reformation, that the hour of God's judgment is come. This judgment is a time well known and precisely defined in Daniel and John's chronological prophecies.

The second message cannot be given before the first is. The second message announces the fall of Babylon, and a voice is heard from heaven afterward, saying, "Come out of her, My people" (18:4). How absurd it is to apply this to after the second advent of Christ, since all His people, both living and dead, are at that time caught up to meet Him in the air to be with Him forever (see 1 Thess. 4:17). They cannot be called out of Babylon after this. Christ does not take them to Babylon, but to the Father's house, where there are many mansions (see John 14:2, 3).

At a glance, the difficulty of this alternative interpretation becomes clearer, since the third angel's message being followed by a future age shows this difficulty. This message warns against the worship of the beast, which refers, as many have discovered, to papal Rome. However, this beast is destroyed and given to the burning flame when Christ returns (see Dan. 7:11; 2 Thess. 2:8). He goes into the lake of fire to no longer disturb God's saints (see Rev. 19:20).

Why should we be concerned with applying a message against the worship of the beast at a time when the beast has ceased to exist, thus making the worship of it impossible? In Revelation 14:13, a blessing is pronounced upon the dead who die in the Lord from the time the threefold message begins to be given. This is a complete demonstration of the fact that the message must be given before the first resurrection, for after that event, all who have a part therein cannot die anymore.

Therefore, we dismiss this view concerning the future age as unscriptural and impossible. If the message has not been proclaimed in the past and cannot be proclaimed after Christ returns, to what period can we apply it except the present generation, since we are obviously in the last days just preceding the second advent? The message proclaims that the hour of God's judgment has come, and this judgment pertains to the closing of the work of salvation for the world.

The apostle Paul reasoned with Felix, the Roman governor, about a "judgment to come" (Acts 24:25) and proclaimed to his hearers on Mars Hill that God had "appointed a day, in the which he will judge the world in righteousness by *that* man whom he hath ordained" (17:31, KJV). The prophecy of the 2,300 days/years of Daniel 8 and 9 pointed to this judgment hour. It extends from 457 BC to AD 1844. The prediction of the fall of Babylon finds its ultimate, last-day fulfillment in the departure of Protestantism at large from the purity and simplicity of the gospel (see Rev. 14:4).

This message was first preached by the Millerite movement in the summer of 1833 and applied to the churches that rejected the first angel's message about the judgment. It will have increased relevance as we draw nearer to the return of Christ.

> Then a third angel followed them, saying with a loud voice, "If anyone worships the beast and his image, and receives *his* mark on his forehead or on his hand, he himself shall also drink of the wine of the wrath of God, which is poured out full strength into the cup of His indignation. He shall be tormented with fire and brimstone in the presence of the holy angels and in the presence of the Lamb. And the smoke of their torment ascends forever and ever; and they have no rest day or night, who worship the beast and his image, and whoever receives the mark of his name." (Rev. 14:9–11)

History reveals that this beast power received a deadly wound. History also reveals that the deadly wound was healed. It was inflicted in 1798 when Berthier, a French General in Napoleon's army, arrested the pope and took him prisoner to France, where he eventually died. It was healed when, in 1929, the Italian President, Bonito Mussolini, met with the pope, who up to that time was head of the church *in absentia*, and they signed documents that returned to the pope power and full authority to again govern Vatican City.

Published in all the major papers of the world, Scripture recorded that these events would occur, and prophecy was fulfilled on time. As these events were occurring as predicted, another power was coming into existence in the new world, which the Bible called a lamblike beast. This new nation has, as foretold, gained worldwide prominence and power.

The Bible says that it will give its power to the first beast (see Rev. 13). Keep your eyes focused on events as prophecy continues to unfold. The signs are taking place almost on a daily basis. God's Bible prophecy clock is always on time. His Word is certain, sure, and can never fail. Today, there are forces working to bring about changes to the Constitution of the United States of America. Today, one vital arm of the Federal Government, the Supreme Court, is, at a two-thirds ratio, dominated by one religious organization. Whenever church and state unite, the former invariably uses the power of the latter to enforce its will—religious domination.

History will repeat itself. The beast power is actively working to bring about radical changes that will do away with the freedom to exercise individual conscience. Changes have already been put in place to remove certain liberties that we have taken for granted. These removals will enable this beast power to speak and cause as many as will not worship its image to be killed.

> And he causes all, both small and great, rich and poor, free and slave, to receive a mark on their right hand or on their

> foreheads, and that no one may buy or sell except one who has the mark or the name of the beast, or the number of his name. Here is wisdom. Let him who has understanding calculate the number of the beast, for it is the number of a man: His number *is* 666. (Revelation 13:16–18)

I am not saying that people will be going around with a number stamped on their foreheads or palms of their hands. The hand is used to earn a living, and the forehead is the seat of thought. The beast will seek to enforce laws against the freedom to worship as one's conscience dictates. One way it will do this is by refusing to allow free trade or commerce to occur unless one worships as the beast orders.

In the past, the church has enforced its will on those who seek to worship God freely, and this will happen again. The Bible informs us that this power will again use force. In the past, this false church persecuted those who refused to do as it commanded. It confiscated homes and other personal property and tortured and put to death many "heretics" on the pretext that they were doing God's will.

The Lord has never forced anyone. On the other hand, the beast power has done and will again do just that. That is how this satanic power has always operated. Today, there are many who refuse to believe that these things will occur. The Scripture says otherwise. Look around, for even as this is being written, there are forces at work seeking to take away basic freedoms. If we would only open our eyes, even in the very recent past, we would see things are afoot, seeking to steal fundamental liberties. While we are looking for prophetic fulfillment to take place overseas, it is currently happening right under our noses.

We need to sharpen our awareness because the hood is being pulled over our eyes on a daily basis. God has given messages in His Word to prepare us if we would only be attentive to them. Ever since the devil introduced sin into our world, he has been actively causing the devolution of our planet. Mankind has been foolishly seeking its destruction ever since. Satan has always wanted to be worshipped. That is why he caused rebellion in heaven, right in the paradise of our Creator.

God is allowing the devil to show all his cards. The devil was defeated at the cross. If he had understood what the Lord was doing, he would not have encouraged evil people to crucify the eternal Son of God. He intends to cause the human race to be permanently lost. However, God had a plan from before the foundation of the world was laid. It was His eternal mystery from everlasting, first outlined in Genesis 3:15. Christ gave His life on Calvary's cross to redeem all who will come to Him and be saved.

While humanity, urged on by the devil, is seeking self-destruction, God's design to restore all things is moving forward to its final culmination. How will it all end? Wait patiently and look for the waymarks. "You search the Scriptures, for in them you think you have eternal life; and these are they which testify of Me" (John 5:39). Jesus, the Creator, Author, and Giver of life, was speaking to the leaders, and they were rejecting Him because their eyes were blind.

People taking the lives of others is now so commonplace that no one appears to be shocked or give much thought to these occurrences anymore.

Do not reject the Savior today. He is still calling people to come to Him and be saved. The Word of God is true. He gave the prophet Daniel visions that, over the centuries, have unfolded just as He told him they would. According to these prophecies, we are now living in the final period of earth's history. We have been living in the period of the ten toes of the divided Roman Empire. Anyone who refers to God's Word will see how everything precisely fits into place.

> You watched while a stone was cut out without hands, which struck the image on its feet of iron and clay, and broke them in pieces. Then the iron, the clay, the bronze,

the silver, and the gold were crushed together, and became like chaff from the summer threshing floors; the wind carried them away so that no trace of them was found. And the stone that struck the image became a great mountain and filled the whole earth. This *is* the dream. Now we will tell the interpretation of it before the king. You, O king, *are* a king of kings. For the God of heaven has given you a kingdom, power, strength, and glory; and wherever the children of men dwell, or the beasts of the field and the birds of the heaven, He has given *them* into your hand, and has made you ruler over them all— you *are* this head of gold. But after you shall arise another kingdom inferior to yours; then another; a third kingdom of bronze, which shall rule over all the earth. And the fourth kingdom shall be as strong as iron… Whereas you saw the feet… And *as* the toes of the feet *were* partly of iron and partly of clay, *so* the kingdom shall be partly strong and partly fragile. As you saw iron mixed with ceramic clay, they will mingle with the seed of men; but they will not adhere to one another, just as iron does not mix with clay. And in the days of these kings the God of heaven will set up a kingdom which shall never be destroyed; and the kingdom shall not be left to other people; it shall break in pieces and consume all these kingdoms, and it shall stand forever. Inasmuch as you saw that the stone was cut out of the mountain without hands, and that it broke in pieces the iron, the bronze, the clay, the silver; and the gold—the great God has made known to the king what will come to pass after this. The dream is certain, and its interpretation is sure. (Daniel 2:34–45)

Today, we are living in a period of history when, as we observe the signs, seasons, and conditions in various cultures, everything seems to point to the predicted time when, unless the Creator God intervenes, mankind will self-destruct. For example, look at what is happening in the Middle East. Observe the changes occurring in other areas of our world. It seems that every nation is having difficulty feeding their citizens. Things that perhaps no one would ever believe to be possible are happening daily.

Friends, read and listen to the Word of God. Prophetic realization is happening, even as you go about your daily affairs. Scripture is being fulfilled! We hear of wars and rumors of wars. People seem to have lost all concern for the value of human life. It looks like everyone has to have the most powerful firearm available. It is a marvel that more people do not shoot off their own hands and feet. People taking the lives of others is now so commonplace that no one appears to be shocked or give much thought to these occurrences anymore.

CHAPTER 13

Do Not Neglect Salvation

God has given His children reasons to exercise faith in and faithfulness to Him. He has always encouraged His people not to neglect His offer of salvation through His only Son, Jesus Christ. It is left to each person to take heed. Our Christian journey is a walk of faith in our Lord and Savior. Our wonderful Father desires that all humanity be saved, and He has done everything possible for all who are willing to be saved.

There is evidence of this throughout the entire Scriptures. The problem is that not everyone is willing to listen, take heed, and trust and obey God. Jesus Christ, in coming down to earth to be our Savior, took on humanity, but not the sin-nature that we all have inherited from Adam, the first man. "Therefore, it is also contained in the Scripture, 'Behold, I lay in Zion A chief cornerstone, elect, precious, And he who believes on Him will by no means be put to shame.' Therefore, to you who believe, *He* [Christ] *is* precious; but to those who are disobedient, 'The stone which the builders rejected Has become the chief cornerstone,' and, 'A stone of stumbling And a rock of offense'" (1 Peter 2:6–8).

The passage goes on to explain why some stumble (see also Isa. 8:14; 28:16; 40:6–8; 53:9; Ps. 118:22):

> They stumble, being disobedient to the word, to which they also were appointed. But you *are* a chosen generation, a royal priesthood, a holy nation, His own special people, that you may proclaim the praises of Him who called you out of darkness into His marvelous light; who once *were*

not a people but *are* now the people of God, who had not obtained mercy but have obtained mercy. (1 Peter 8–10)

In the time of the flood, God gave Noah a message of warning and redemption, which he preached for 120 years, yet only he and his family were saved when the flood came. For that entire period, the people stood around and mocked old Noah while he built the ark according to the plans God gave him. They never saw rain before. Up to the time, the earth and vegetation were watered by the dew that came up from the ground.

Therefore, when Noah told the people that the earth was going to be destroyed by a flood, they laughed and scoffed at him. They continued in their sins, debauched lifestyles, and rebellion against the Creator of all things. As we look around today, we see the same thing happening in all cultures, as we have read in Matthew 24 and 25. There is a willingness to kill and destroy human lives, with little or no consequence, on all sides. It may not matter to mankind, but God is keeping a record.

> *Today, the greatest earthly power is fast declining as it loses the respect of other nations.*

In the days of Noah, they mocked the Lord of heaven and earth, just as they are doing today. There are many in positions of authority who look the other way and pretend not to notice, but He sees their negligence and holds them responsible. All these conditions in the world point to the soon return of Jesus Christ.

Today, the greatest earthly power is fast declining as it loses the respect of other nations. This began years ago when the government changed the curriculum by banning prayer in schools and removing the Ten Commandments from public places. Almighty God sees this, and even though some religious organizations keep silent in order not to ruffle feathers, their guilt remains. It is, bluntly speaking, a great sin against the God of heaven and earth.

However, there are far more worst things to come, and people will still turn a blind eye. They did the same thing during World War II, and mark my words, history is bound to repeat itself, mistakes and all. God gave a special message through the prophet Daniel: "And in the days of these kings the God of heaven set up a kingdom which shall never be destroyed; and the kingdom shall not be left to other people; it shall break in pieces and consume all these kingdoms, and it shall stand forever (2:44).

We can see changes in the natural world, yet humanity insists on going their head-strong way and continues sliding down to a cloudless, eternal night. As it was in past civilizations, so now mankind persists along its path to destruction. However, "The Lord is not slack concerning *His* promise, as some count slackness, but is long suffering toward us, not willing that any should perish but that all should come to repentance" (2 Peter 3:9).

After everything God, in Christ, has done to save humanity, Paul asks this vital question: "how shall we escape if we neglect so great a salvation, which at the first began to be spoken by the Lord, and was confirmed to us by those who heard *Him*" (Heb. 2:3)? This book lists six stern warnings given to the ancients who neglected to heed them, in spite of everything He did for their salvation, and, as a result, missed the promised blessings.

They began drifting away from God's love and compassion for them. This was followed by doubting that He cared for their welfare. Soon, the nation turned deaf ears to the repeated warnings that the prophets gave. The next backslide was that some began yearning to return to Egypt and a life of slavery from which the Lord had miraculously delivered them. Oh, how they stubbornly began despising the divine promises that He would fulfill if they would only hold fast and press forward in their journey to the Promised Land! The patriarchs and prophets of old who did hold fast have gone on before us and left reports of their perseverance as we, now on the borders of the heavenly Canaan, are nearing home.

Bible scholars are not in full agreement as to who wrote the Book of Hebrews. Some lean to one option, and others to another. However, it is important to realize that this valuable tome, which lists the exploits of those who, under God's providence, came to realize that in all their experiences, the divine mystery was revealed through the incarnate Christ, who came from heaven to redeem us all from the devil's trap. This was a plan that the Triune God devised before they laid the foundations of the world.

Satan used a variety of methods of ensnaring Christ at different times and in different ways to defeat the plan for the redemption of humanity. It is important to realize that no earthly power can ever defeat God's purposes. Though there's the question of who wrote Hebrews and its historical exploits of those warriors of faith, the Holy Spirit is definitely the Author. He is still urging valiant laborers in these last days of earth's history to press on towards the mark of the upward call of God in Christ. Let us, therefore, press forward by His power as we realize that we are nearing home.

The journey is almost over, and the patriarchs of ages past left us a written account that charges us to press forward. Through the eyes of faith, the goal is in sight. The night is almost over; the dawn is coming nigh. King Immanuel beckons us. Soon we will hear the trumpet sounding. He is surely coming again. Let's keep our eyes on the eastern skies and hold the fort in the meantime. Do not neglect God's free salvation offered through His Son, our Lord and Savior Jesus Christ. He will keep his promise. The changing times testify that end-time prophecies are fast unfolding.

CHAPTER 14

The Holy and the Profane

Let my prayer be set before You *as* incense, The lifting up of my hands *as* the evening sacrifice. Set a guard, O LORD, over my mouth; keep watch over the door of my lips. Do not incline my heart to any evil thing, To practice wicked works With men who work iniquity; And do not let me eat of their delicacies. Let the righteous strike me; *It shall be* a kindness. And let him rebuke me; *It shall be* as excellent oil; Let my head not refuse it. For still my prayer *is* against the deeds of the wicked. (Psalm 141:2–5)

Incense in the Bible is symbolic of the prayers of the saints. Anything offered to God, such as our monetary offerings or prayers, are to be holy, for our God is Holy, and He wants us to be holy too. He commanded Moses, saying, "Speak to all the congregation of the children of Israel, and say to them: 'You shall be holy, for I the Lord your God *am* holy" (Lev. 19:2).

Lest anyone get the idea that the God in the Old Testament is different from the God in the New Testament, Paul says, "Blessed *be* the God and Father of our Lord Jesus Christ, who has blessed us with every spiritual blessing in the heavenly *places* in Christ, just as He chose us in Him before the foundation of the world, that we should be holy and without blame before Him in love" (Eph. 1:3, 4).

"So it was, that while [Zacharias, the father of John the Baptist] was serving as priest before God in the order of his division, according to the custom of the priesthood, his lot fell to burn incense when he went into the temple of the Lord. And the whole multitude of the people was praying outside at the hour of incense"

> *Today, our prayers are blended (mixed) with the righteousness of Christ. The Holy Spirit carries our prayers as we lift them toward the throne room of God, where Jesus officiates as our Great High Priest.*

(Luke 1:8–10). Today, our prayers are blended (mixed) with the righteousness of Christ. The Holy Spirit carries our prayers as we lift them toward the throne room of God, where Jesus officiates as our Great High Priest.

Let us see what lessons there are for us today from the following passage: "Then Nadab and Abihu, the sons of Aaron, each took his censer and put fire in it, put incense on it, and offered profane fire before the LORD, which He had not commanded them. So fire went out from the LORD and devoured them, and they died before the LORD" (Lev. 10:1, 2). There are many today, even among Christians, who dare to criticize God for this, but the problem is that they overlook several factors. The nation was coming out of 400 years of paganism. The Creator was teaching them how they were to worship Him. He had previously instructed them in what He required of them, for they were to be a kingdom of priests who would be teaching the surrounding heathen nations about the One true God of heaven and earth. They were to abstain from wine and strong drink when they served before the Lord. Nadab and Abihu were willfully disobedient in what they had done, so they could not stand in His presence.

> And Moses said to Aaron, "This is what the LORD spoke, saying: 'By those who come near Me I must be regarded as holy; And before all the people I must be glorified.'" So Aaron held his peace. And Moses said to Aaron, and to Eleazar and Ithamar, his sons, "Do not uncover your heads nor tear your clothes, lest you die, and wrath come upon all the people. But let your brethren, the whole house of Israel, bewail the burning which the LORD has kindled. You shall not go out from the door of the tabernacle of meeting, lest you die, for the anointing oil of the LORD *is* upon you." ...Then the LORD spoke to Aaron, saying: "Do not drink wine or intoxicating drink, you, nor your sons with you, when you go into the tabernacle of meeting, lest you die. *It shall be* a statute forever throughout your generations, that you may distinguish between holy and unholy, and between unclean and clean, and that you may teach the children of Israel all the statutes which the LORD has spoken to them by the hand of Moses." (Leviticus 10:3, 6–11)

God expects people to worship Him as He desires to be worshipped. It is implied that Nadab and Abihu were intoxicated and thus clouded in their thinking, for in verse 9, God reminded Aaron of the command that he and his sons should refrain from strong drink when they served in the temple before Him. It should be noted that when Hannah prayed for a son, whom she promised to return to the Lord for His service, no razor was to "come upon his head" (1 Sam. 1:11). She knew that drinking strong drink was wrong (see vs. 15, 16). After Samuel was born, all his life he drank no strong drink.

Samson's mother was told that she should not drink of the fruit of the vine, for the child which she was to have would be a Nazirite (see Judges 13:3–5). This restriction was also applied to John the Baptist (see Luke 1:15). God will help us if we ask to live holy lives (see Eph. 1:4, 11). "One who turns away his ear from hearing the law, Even his prayer *is* an abomination" (Prov. 28:9).

Every word of God is true. His promises are sure. He keeps and fulfills everything He says. He may, by His infinite wisdom, delay the time of fulfillment, but He is a promise-keeping God who is always loving, kind, and good. "If I regard iniquity in my heart, The Lord will not hear. *But* certainly God has heard *me*; He has attended to the voice of my prayer. Blessed *be* God, Who has not turned away my prayer, Nor His mercy from me" (Ps. 66:18–20)!

Nadab and Abihu's hearts were not right toward God because they were drunk with intoxicating drink, which He had forbidden. Leviticus 10 makes it obvious that they could not distinguish between holy and unholy, clean, and unclean. They were destroyed by the glory of God. He is equally displeased when holy things are treated as common.

Belshazzar, the pagan king of Babylon, commanded that the holy vessels that his grandfather took from the temple in Jerusalem should be brought to him during a night of debauchery, so that his wives and concubines, along with his lords and guests, could drink wine from them. Immediately, the fingers of an unseen hand were seen writing on the wall: "MENE, MENE, TEKEL, UPHARSIN" Daniel was called to interpret the writing. The aged prophet and statesman reminded the king that he was aware of the sacredness of the vessels dedicated to the service of the God of heaven. Then he gave the interpretation: "God has numbered your kingdom, and finished it… You have been weighed in the balances, and found wanting… Your kingdom has been divided…" (5:25–28).

God's judgments are equally sure. In love and mercy, He may choose to delay or postpone the fulfillment, or even reverse it, depending on the people's response, as in the case of Nineveh. However, God's promises are trustworthy.

Belshazzar's doom was sealed, even as the judgment was pronounced. The Medes and Persians were at the gate. Anything that God has set aside as holy must be treated as sacred. Mankind, in willful disobedience, will not escape His judgment. History often repeats itself, and this is predicted to occur in Bible prophecy. We can, with the utmost assurance, look for these events to take place, although the exact time has not been divulged. Having these warnings should sufficiently prepare us ahead of time.

The times and seasons are changing, and we, therefore, should not be surprised if we read the Bible and take heed. Another doom is soon to be pronounced upon the earth. Revelation 18:1–5 speaks of a power that will trample upon the truth of God's commandments and think to change times and laws. This power will attempt to eradicate the Word of God and persecute those who seek to obey Him.

Eventually, doom will be pronounced, on a global scale, upon those who change God's holy law and teach and lead others astray in wrongful conduct. That very night, Belshazzar and those around him were killed. In the entire universe, there is no Being who can compare to the everlasting God, Creator of heaven and earth. He is the only pre-existent One. There is none like Him. He is self-existent and will endure eternally.

> Lord, You have been our dwelling place in all generations. Before the mountains were brought forth, Or ever You had formed the earth and the world, Even from everlasting to everlasting, You *are* God. You turn man to destruction, And say, "Return, O children of men." For a thousand years in Your sight *Are* like yesterday when it is past, And *like* a watch in the night. You carry them away *like* a flood;

They are like a sleep. In the morning they are like grass
which grows up: In the morning it flourishes and grows up;
In the evening it is cut down and withers. (Psalm 90:1–6)

In the book of Isaiah, God asks the question, "Is there a God besides Me" (44:8)? Our mighty Lord is incomparable. There is none who can be compared to Him. Again, God is holy, and He wants us to be holy also. He has created us with the ability to make our own choices. He will never take that attribute from us. He desires us to love Him of our own volition. He wants a reciprocal relationship, and giving Him love is only meaningful if we can withhold it. That is the only kind of love. "Yes, I have loved you with an everlasting love; Therefore with lovingkindness I have drawn you" (Jer. 31:3). God sent His only Son, Jesus Christ, to the cross to prove His love (see John 3:16–18).

God, in Christ, is still calling us to Himself. He says, "Come to Me, all *you* who labor and are heavy laden, and I will give you rest. Take My yoke upon you and learn from Me, for I am gentle and lowly in heart, and you will find rest for your souls. For My yoke *is* easy and My burden is light" (Matt. 11:28–30).

CHAPTER 15

Why Esau Lost His Birthright

Now it happened, as soon as Isaac had finished blessing Jacob, and Jacob had scarcely gone out from the presence of Isaac his father, that Esau his brother came in from his hunting. He also had made savory food, and brought it to his father, and said to his father, "Let my father arise and eat of his son's game, that your soul may bless me." And his father Isaac said to him, "Who *are* you?" So he said, "I *am* your son, your firstborn, Esau." Then Isaac trembled exceedingly, and said, "Who? Where *is* the one who hunted game and brought *it* to me? I ate all *of it* before you came, and I have blessed him—*and* indeed he shall be blessed." When Esau heard the words of his father, he cried with an exceedingly great and bitter cry, and said to his father, "Bless me—me also, O my father!" But he said, "Your brother came with deceit and has taken away your blessing." (Genesis 27:30–35)

As we walk this journey of faith, Christians are to, by the power of the Holy Spirit, avoid all temptations to give in to any form of sin. No one will drift into heaven. "[W]e must through much tribulation enter into the kingdom of God" (Acts 14:22, KJV; see also Matt. 7:21–27; 10:23). Let us draw near. It is not enough to believe in Christ and His priestly ministry in the courts above. Sincere believers will make use of the faculties that heaven has generously provided, by which they "may obtain mercy and find grace to help in time of need" (Heb. 4:16).

Drawing near implies intimate communion and fellowship. Let us consider how to encourage one another in love and good works. Esau is named as an example of one who yielded to besetting sins and passions, denied the grace of God, and lost his birthright. He, although a twin, was the first to come out of the womb and therefore the older of the two brothers. Being the first child carried many privileges. On the death of his father Isaac, Esau would become head of the family.

Esau, like all of us, had flaws. The problem was that he never overcame them, which led to his downfall. He had no interest in spiritual things, but preferred to be out in the woods hunting. He was the favorite son of his father. Jacob, on the other hand, was always around the house and became Rebecca's favorite. Esau allowed appetite to control his actions and, in short, he sold his birthright to his conniving, selfish, and dishonest brother for a bowl of stew.

Esau was a profane person. Afterward, when he realized how he had rejected the blessing in a moment of rashness for a morsel of food, it was too late; the damage had been done. Commentators all agree that "Long years of living for earthly pursuits had deprived Esau of the capacity to bear the more serious responsibilities of life. By his own choice his mind and character had become fixed" (White 1957, p. 486). He cried with bitter tears, but it was in vain.

As ancient Israel came to Mount Sinai and heard the voice of God (see Heb. 12:18–21), so today, Christians, not in a literal but spiritual sense, have come to Mount Sion and are to heed the voice of Jesus (see vs. 22–25). The Hebrews repeatedly failed to heed the voice of Jehovah, and as a result of their stubborn disobedience, only two of those who came out of Egypt, aged twenty years and over, entered the Promised Land.

It was no arbitrary act of God that kept Esau from receiving the inheritance that would otherwise have been his. His character disqualified him from its privileges and responsibilities. When he realized what he had lost, "he cried with a great and exceeding bitter cry" (Gen. 27:34).

The giving of the law at Mount Sinai was attended with a most impressive display of the power of God. Never before or since has the world witnessed anything so awe-inspiring. Paul speaks figuratively of living Christians being assembled around the Lord's throne in heaven—a great gathering of the church invisible. Our heavenly Father and Savior Jesus Christ have always given warnings before judgment comes, and His punishments are always balanced with mercy, justice, and truth. It has always been so because "God is love." That is the mark of His character.

Ancient Israel came to the actual Mount Sinai, heard the voice of God, felt the mountain quake, and saw the fire and, as they traveled from Egypt, smoke (see Ex. 19:9–25). Christians today have not come to that mountain that can be touched, but by the Holy Spirit, we have come into the presence of Christ and are to obey Him.

> *It was no arbitrary act of God that kept Esau from receiving the inheritance that would otherwise have been his. His character disqualified him from its privileges and responsibilities.*

In other words, we are not to repeat the same mistakes that ancient Israel made as they traveled from Egypt to Canaan. We have these lessons as examples to us in this last generation. We, however, will have no second opportunity to repent if we make the same mistakes. Like Esau, we will only find that no amount of tearful regret will serve any useful purpose. The only recourse left to us will be a fearful looking forward to the day of the Lord.

As Esau came to realize, if we fail to prepare to meet Jesus at His return, we can only expect judgment. "For the promise is to you and to your children, and to all who are afar off, as many as the Lord our God will call" (Acts 2:39). Repent and come to Jesus while the opportunity is available. If this gospel of the kingdom is preached in all the world for a witness, He has promised, "the end will come."

Esau lost the blessing because he had no interest in a life of godly conduct. He treated the blessing that would have come to him at the death of his father and everything it was meant to represent lightly. This firstborn son was a very cunning hunter, outdoorsy, rough, and adventurous. Jacob was an unassuming man and tended to be an amiable, pious, and cultured person. He developed the character of a stable person with the soundness of judgment that comes with maturity. Isaac, the father, was blind and loved Esau, irrespective of his character qualifications for family leadership, while Rebecca, the mother, loved Jacob.

At the birth of these twins, God told Rebecca that the younger would rule the older. Somehow, she felt obliged to believe that she needed to assist Him. When she heard Isaac tell Esau to prepare the stew so that he could eat it and then bless him before he died, she feared that he would become the head of the family. If only we would wait upon God to work out His purposes in our lives, we would avoid a lot of problems. By interfering instead of waiting, Rebecca was obliged to send her favorite son to her brother's house for his safety, never to see him again before she died.

Esau's unsuitability to someday be the head of the family became more apparent as he matured. The extent to which he allowed his actions to be ruled by his appetite reflects his unpreparedness to be a spiritual or even titular leader.

> Now Jacob cooked a stew; and Esau came in from the field, and he *was* weary. And Esau said to Jacob, "Please feed me with that same red *stew*, for I *am* weary." Therefore his name was called Edom [meaning "red"]. But Jacob said, "Sell me your birthright as of this day." And Esau said, "Look, I *am* about to die; so what *is* this birthright to me?" Then Jacob said, "Swear to me as of this day." So he swore to him, and sold his birthright to Jacob. And Jacob gave Esau bread and stew of lentils; then he ate and drank, arose, and went his way. Thus Esau despised *his* birthright. (Genesis 25:29–34)

To Esau, the only thing of value was the momentary satisfaction of appetite. The future, spiritual blessings that would have been his by birth seemed remote, unreal, and in the distant future. He tended to give thought only to the moment; instant gratification was all that mattered to him. He gave no thought to future blessings. In this, he showed himself to be a profane irreligious, person, insensible to spiritual things. He cared for nothing but the indulgence of basic desires. Like the dumb brute of the field, he based his decisions only on the sensual considerations of the moment.

The extent to which a person is willing to sacrifice present desires for future good is an accurate measure of emotional and spiritual maturity. On this basis, only those of utmost integrity and high, God-fearing ideals can ever become fully developed, for they alone are ready and willing to forfeit all this life has to offer, that they may be accounted worthy of the life to come (see 2 Cor. 4:17, 18; Phil. 3:7–15; Acts 20:24; Luke 20:34, 35; Heb. 11:10).

The trifling way in which Esau sold his birthright for a dish of lentils—a mere bowl of stew—demonstrated his unpreparedness to become heir to the gracious promises of God. While Jacob's conduct cannot be condoned, that of Esau is deserving of the most severe consideration. Jacob repented and was forgiven; Esau was beyond forgiveness because his repentance consisted only of regret for the results of his rash act, not the act itself (see Heb. 12:16, 17).

Without much thought, Esau settled for mere momentary satisfaction, ignoring the blessings that might accrue from timely patience and considerable, long-term benefits to himself and others. Hasty and rash decisions often result in sorrowful consequences. That ought to be a lesson to us when we are tempted to become impatient, rather than wait upon the Lord.

> Therefore we also, since we are surrounded by so great a cloud of witnesses, let us lay aside every weight, and the sin which so easily ensnares *us*, and let us run with endurance

the race that is set before us, looking unto Jesus, the author and finisher of *our* faith, who for the joy that was set before Him endured the cross, despising the shame, and has sat down at the right hand of the throne of God. For consider Him who endured such hostility from sinners against Himself, lest you become weary and discouraged in your souls. You have not yet resisted to bloodshed, striving against sin. And you have forgotten the exhortation which speaks to you as to sons: "My son, do not despise the chastening of the LORD, Nor be discouraged when you are rebuked by Him; For whom the LORD loves He chastens, And scourges every son whom he receives." (Hebrews 12:1–6)

CHAPTER 16

And If this Gospel Is Preached

Jesus came to Nazareth, where He had been raised, and as was His custom, He went into the synagogue on the Sabbath day and stood up to read. He was handed the book of the prophet Isaiah, and when He opened it, He found the place where it was written, "The Spirit of the LORD *is* upon Me, Because He has appointed Me To preach the gospel to *the* poor; He has sent Me to heal the brokenhearted, To preach liberty to *the* captives And recovery of sight to *the* blind, *To* set at liberty those who are oppressed; To proclaim the acceptable year of the LORD" (Luke 4:18, 19).

This was the mission statement of Jesus Christ when He came to earth. At age twelve, His earthly parents took Him to attend the Passover in Jerusalem. On their homeward journey, they realized that they had lost him in the crowd. They initially thought He was with others from Nazareth. On returning to Jerusalem after three days, they found Him in the temple in meaningful discussion with the leaders, asking and answering questions. In addressing His parents' deep concern, He replied, "Why did you seek Me? Did you not know that I must be about My Father's business" (Luke 2:49)? Scripture says, "And Jesus increased in wisdom and stature, and in favor with God and men" (v. 52).

When Jesus was thirty years old, John the Baptist, His forerunner, was preaching by the Jordan river and calling people to repentance from sin. Although they were cousins, they had never met before. He saw Jesus coming toward him and announced:

> "Behold! The Lamb of God who takes away the sin of the world! This is He of whom I said, 'After me comes a Man who is preferred before me, for He was before me.' I did not know Him; but that He should be revealed to Israel, therefore I came baptizing with water." And John bore witness, saying, "I saw the Spirit descending from heaven like a dove, and He remained upon Him. I did not know Him, but He who sent me to baptize with water said to me, 'Upon whom you see the Spirit descending, and remaining on Him, this is He who baptizes with the Holy Spirit.' And I have seen and testified that this is the Son of God." (John 1:29–34)

Jesus had no sin. God's miracle of the virgin-birth incarnation ensured that His Son would indeed come to earth fully human yet fully divine. If there was even one spot of sin in Him, He could not have been the spotless Lamb of God who would die for the sins of all mankind. This was the greatest, most astounding miracle of the Triune God, planned from before the foundation of the world.

Christ needed no repentance. You and I need to repent of our sins. We were born in sin and shaped in iniquity. The Son of God had not one iota of sin Him. That is the reason that the lambs that were set apart for sacrifice had to be carefully selected. Each lamb, or whatever animal, chosen for sacrifice represented Jesus the Lamb of God, who would come to die for the sins of the world.

Every person who has ever lived, except Jesus, has been stained because of Adam's sin. Christ came to earth to be God's sacrifice for the sins of the whole world. His name was to be "Jesus," for He would "save" His people from their sins, though He would also be called "Immanuel," meaning "God with us." It is inconceivable that there are those who claim to be schooled in the deeper meaning of the gospel and teaching others, yet deny the virgin birth. It seems quite sacrilegious, as if they have no fear or reverence for God, though they ought to.

Jesus was baptized to fully identify Himself with humanity. He came to earth as God's Substitute for all mankind's sins. To be a complete sacrifice and High Priest for us, He needed to be able to identify with us so that He can understand our weaknesses and represent us at His Father's throne. Jesus, therefore, asked John the Baptist to baptize Him.

At first, John refused, stating that he was the one who needed to be baptized. Jesus explained to him that it was necessary to fulfill all righteousness. John then complied with the request and baptized Him. As Jesus was coming up out of the water, a voice came from heaven, saying, "This is My beloved Son, in whom I am well pleased" (Matt. 3:17). The Holy Spirit, in the form of a dove, illuminated the Savior.

Everything that occurred had tremendous significance. Every step was a preparation for the work which Jesus was sent to earth to perform for the salvation of mankind, as well as His function as a high priest and intercessor before the throne of God in the heavenly sanctuary, even now as I am writing this. Jesus is mediating at the mercy seat for His people, His priesthood is not as much of the order of Aaron, which was temporary, but of the order of Melchizedek, thus being everlasting.

Melchizedek met and later blessed Abraham as he was returning from the slaughter of the kings. "Now consider how great this man [Melchizedek] *was*, to whom even the patriarch Abraham gave a tenth [tithe] of the spoils" (Heb. 7:4). Many believe that Melchizedek was a theophany of the pre-incarnate Christ. The name "Melchizedek" means "king of righteousness" and "king of Salem (Peace)" (see vs. 1, 2). Jesus is *the* King of Peace. He is God of gods.

When Jesus died, the sins that He carried to Calvary's cross were our sins, not His. Our Savior had no sin of His own. My sins, your sins, and the sins of every person who has ever lived or will ever live were put upon Him. He shed His precious blood for the sins of every person in the whole world, past, present, and future. Even the sins of those who rejected Jesus and nailed Him to the cross were put upon Him, but not into Him. He did all of this so that we may have eternal life (see John 3:16–18).

> *When Jesus died, the sins that He carried to Calvary's cross were our sins, not His.*

Those who refuse God's gift of salvation, offered through the death, burial, and resurrection of Jesus Christ, will have to bear the penalty for their sins. The problem is that they will not have a savior to be their sin-bearer after their probation is closed. There are some folks going around telling those who now refuse to accept Jesus' gift that they will have a second chance after He comes back. That is a mistaken view. The Bible is clear. Now is the opportune time. Today is the day of salvation.

Just as the people in Noah's day waited until God had shut the door of the ark, and thus were too late to be saved, so will it be when Jesus returns, and there will not be a second chance.

> Then the angel said to her, "Do not be afraid, Mary, for you have found favor with God. And behold, you

> will conceive in your womb and bring forth a Son, and shall call His name JESUS. He will be great, and will be called the Son of the Highest; and the Lord God will give Him the throne of His father David. And He will reign over the house of Jacob forever, and of His kingdom there will be no end." Then Mary said to the angel, "How can this be, since I do not know a man?" And the angel answered and said to her, *"The* Holy Spirit will come upon you, and the power of the Highest will overshadow you; therefore, also, that Holy One who is to be born will be called the Son of God.... For with God nothing will be impossible." (Luke 1:30–35, 37)

If Jesus was not who He said He was, it would have been impossible for so many of the prophecies about Him to have been fulfilled. None of those prophecies would have been fulfilled in only this One Man if He had not been virgin born. Throughout history, Jesus has been the only Being who was virgin born. He is the only Savior, and there will be no other.

Look around you and see for yourselves how rapidly Bible prophecy is being fulfilled. Does anyone doubt that we are in the last days of this earth's history? God sent an angel to tell the prophet Daniel, "shut up the words, and seal the book until the time of the end; many shall run to and fro, and knowledge shall increase" (12:4). Does anyone doubt that people are running to and fro all over this world? Is there no evidence that knowledge is increasing at a very rapid rate? Jesus is coming soon!

Jesus came to earth to be God's sacrificial lamb, slain for sinners. Why did He do this? His love impelled Him. When the very creatures whom He made turned against Him, He reacted with forgiving love and surrendered the life of His only Son. If we neglect so great a salvation, what then will we do?

Israel turned against obeying God's plan for their wellbeing. He repeatedly forgave them and called them to repent, but they would not. Finally, He sent His only Son, His most treasured gift, thinking they would surely repent, but instead, the leaders refused to hear Him and turned Him over to be crucified, saying, in so many words, "Away with Jesus, give us Barabbas."

Pilate asked with profound surprise, "Why, what evil has He done?" He found no fault in Him. He then "took water and washed *his* hands before the multitude, saying, 'I am innocent of the blood of this just Person. You see *to it*.' And all the people answered and said, 'His blood *be* on us and on our children.' Then he released Barabbas to them; and when he had scourged Jesus, he delivered *Him* to be crucified" (Matt. 27:23–26).

Jesus declared that He gave up His life by He own choice. "Therefore My Father loves Me, because I lay down My life that I may take it again. No one takes it from Me, but I lay it down of Myself" (John 10:17, 18). He indicated that if He had chosen to do so, He could have called twelve legions of angels to set Him free. Jesus came to earth with the express purpose of giving His life to redeem all mankind from sin.

What made God offer Himself as such a sacrifice? It was divine love. There was no other way by which lost humanity could have been redeemed from sin and rebellion. It was love that caused the Son of God to give His life as an offering for sin (see Eph. 5:2). The Father, through Jesus Christ, saves all sinners by His grace. Salvation is entirely His work through the gift of His Son. There is nothing we can add. All anyone can do is accept this gift. In the entire universe, there is no other savior.

Before His death, burial, resurrection, and return to heaven, Jesus promised that "if I go to prepare a place for you, I will come again to receive you to Myself; that where I Am, *there* you [all who choose to turn from sin and rebellion and turn to God in Christ] may be also" (John 14:3). There are many who are looking forward to the second coming of Jesus.

Considering all the Old Testament prophecies about Jesus, the Son of God, that were fulfilled, as well as the signs in Matthew 24 and 25 that we see taking place throughout the world around us, we can be sure that Jesus will come again as He promised. Matthew 24:14 still needs to be fulfilled, but in Matthew 28:18–20, a related passage, He promised that

He would be with us throughout our labors for Him, and His promises are sure.

Jesus said that no one knows when His coming will be. Only God the Father knows (see Matt. 24:36; Mark 13:32). He gave many signs in nature, the business world, scientific world, and elsewhere. If people still doubt, just as in the days of Noah, that will not prevent the return of our Savior. Now is the accepted time. Today, if you will hear His voice, harden not your hearts. No one will be able to say they never knew of the love of God. It is difficult to deny the voice of the Holy Spirit.

Today, if you will hear His voice, do not harden your hearts. God has done everything possible to save us from the fires of the last day. Each person must choose. His promises are certain. His creation is crying out for His return. Before He went back to heaven, Jesus told his followers to hold fast until He came to earth again. One way or another, each person is making a choice. God's love is broad and deep. He is calling to everyone, "Come unto Me and be saved!" Jesus said, "Behold, I am coming quickly! Hold fast…" (Rev. 3:11).

CHAPTER 17

Jesus, the "I Am" God with Us

> But all things that are exposed are made manifest by the light, for whatever makes manifest is light. Therefore He says: "Awake, you who sleep, Arise from the dead, And Christ will give you light." See then that you walk circumspectly, not as fools but as wise, redeeming the time, because the days are evil. Therefore do not be unwise, but understand what the will of the Lord *is*. And do not be drunk with wine, in which is dissipation; but be filled with the Spirit… (Ephesians 5:13–18)

Collins Dictionary defines the word "dissipation" as follows: "scattering; waste; squandering; frivolous way of life."

Many see Jesus of Nazareth as a teacher, wise man, and even a Jewish seer who was cruelly treated. He was unjustly punished and suffered an undeserved death. That is as far as many people believe, and no more. However, is there more to the historical Jesus than this? So much has been written about Jesus the Nazarene. Wars have been fought in His name. The stories never seem to end. Nevertheless, there are many who still doubt. If He was really God in the flesh, how was this so? This appears to be the most neglected concept that a lot of people have difficulty understanding.

From early childhood, Jesus certainly did not doubt that He was the Son of God in the flesh. He regarded Himself as far more than an ordinary man or good teacher. At twelve years old, His earthly parents took Him to the Passover celebrations in Jerusalem and, thinking He was with other members of the group traveling back to Nazareth afterward, left Him there.

Three days later, they returned and found Him in the temple in earnest discussion that astounded the rabbis and learned teachers of the law. When they asked Him why He did not leave with the group, He responded, "Did you not know that I must be about My Father's business" (Luke 2:49)?

Over the centuries, many have doubtfully delved into the history and evidence presented about Jesus. Many started as skeptics, but, by the end of their study, came away convinced that He is indeed the Son of God, clothed in humanity. Some critics have gone so far as to claim that the record has been fabricated. However, this is historically impossible because of the reasons we shall see as we progress (see also chapter 4 of this book). There are approximately three hundred prophecies concerning the Messiah in the Old Testament, and all have met their fulfillment in One Person—Jesus Christ. The likelihood of this is 1 in 100 sextillions (ten to the twenty-third power).

Immediately after the death and resurrection of Jesus, the Christian church came into existence and grew explosively, based on the conviction that He was indeed God and Israel's long-expected Messiah. One of His close followers, Simon Peter, was moved by the Holy Spirit to preach a stirring sermon about Jesus raising from the dead and confirming His divinity and designation as the Christ (Anointed One) of God, whom the leaders and people crucified (see Acts 2:14–36; also Gen. 3:15).

The followers of Jesus heard Him speak of His body as the temple, which, if it were torn down, He would raise in three days. However, the Jewish leaders and even the disciples presumed He was speaking of the beautiful Jewish temple built by Herod the Great. The women went to the tomb on Sunday to finish embalming the body, a work that was left unfinished on crucifixion Friday, as it was the preparation day before the Sabbath. After the crucifixion, the leaders of the Jews recalled that Jesus had spoken of being raised from the dead.

Therefore, they went to Pilate and begged him to appoint soldiers to guard the tomb so that His disciples wouldn't steal the body and claim that a resurrection had taken place (see Matt. 27:64). At the same time, the disciples went into hiding, fearful that the Romans and leaders of the Jews would find them and also put them to death. Snatching the body was the last thing on their minds. The reality is that Jesus of Nazareth is God in the flesh.

After His resurrection, God chose women to be the human messengers to tell the disciples what happened. The culture at that time in history was that women could not give testimony in court, for it carried little weight. If Jesus was not God, and if there had been no resurrection, there would have been no basis for the founding of the Christian church. He commanded the disciples to remain in Jerusalem for the coming of the Holy Spirit.

If the resurrection had not occurred, then it would have shown that Jesus was not God. There would have been no credible reason for the sermon that Peter preached; there would have been no descent of the Holy Spirit; neither would there have been any reason for His followers to risk their lives for a lie. Jesus' claims would have been invalidated.

His resurrection and the coming of the Holy Spirit gave power to the founding of the Christian church and the evangelizing thrust of the gospel, which "turned the world upside down".

Addressing this very issue, the apostle Paul later stated that if Christ had not emerged from the grave and ascended to heaven, then Christians would be the most pitiful people, for they would have had no foundation on which to anchor their faith. They would have had no basis for the hope that is in them and or any sound reason to willingly give their lives for something they knew to be false. Jesus rising from the dead is proof that He is indeed the Son of God. His resurrection and the coming of the Holy Spirit gave power to the founding of the Christian church and the evangelizing thrust of the gospel, which "turned the world upside down" (Acts 17:6).

One of the boldest statements Jesus made in declaring to be God was when He told the Pharisees, "before Abraham was, I AM" (John 8:52). This statement, in the English language, may appear confusing. However, in the Hebrew or Aramaic tongue, which Jesus spoke, He was making the claim that caused the people to attempt to stone Him, thinking He was guilty of blasphemy. He was identifying Himself as the One whom the Jews knew as the God in the Old Testament and laying claim to have existed before Abraham did, being the God who Abraham, Isaac, and Jacob knew.

He is the same God who met Moses in the burning bush. "Then Moses said to God, 'Indeed, *when* I come to the children of Israel and say to them, "The God of your fathers has sent me to you," and they say to me, "What *is* His name?" what shall I say to them?' And God said to Moses, 'I AM WHO I AM.' And He said, 'Thus you shall say to the children of Israel, "I AM has sent me to you"'" (Ex. 3:13, 14). Jesus claimed to be this same Being, the God of Abraham, Isaac, and Jacob (see v. 15), and rightfully so. The Creator and Savior, the promised Messiah of Genesis 3:15, for whom the Jews had waited so long, came to them, but they failed to recognize Him. They expected a king who would free them from Roman oppression and restore the Davidic monarchy.

"I AM" and the abbreviated, Hebrew equivalent *YHWH* (Yaw'-way) are the names of God that infer absolute timelessness and self-existence. Although it is impossible to pronounce the latter correctly because when the scribes came to the full meaning of it, they felt such reverence for the name of God that they dared not completely write it out.

Revelation 1:8 contains distinctive applications for Jesus, whose existence is eternal and everlasting. He is the same Being who says, "I *am* the LORD [*YHWH*], that *is* My name; and My glory I will not give to another, Nor My praise to carved images" (Isa. 42:8) and "I *am* the First and I *am* the Last; Besides Me *there is* no God" (44:6).

Dr. Norman Geisler, in his book *Christian Apologetics*, declares, "In view of the fact that the Jehovah of the Jewish Old Testament would not give His name, honor and glory to another, it is little wonder that the words and deeds of Jesus of Nazareth drew stones and cries of blasphemy from first century Jews. The very things that the Jehovah of the Old Testament claimed for Himself Jesus of Nazareth also claimed" (p. 331).

Geisler lists some ways Jesus equated Himself with *YHWH* of the Old Testament: Jesus said of Himself, "I am the Good Shepherd," (John 10:11). David, Israel's ¼ shepherd king wrote: "The LORD [YHWH] is my Shepherd" Psalm 23: 1; Jesus claimed to be Judge of all men and nations, John 5:22, 27; Joel also says, "The LORD [YHWH] will sit to judge all nations" Joel 3:12. Jesus said, "I am the Light of the world" John 8:12. Isaiah 60:19 says: "The LORD will be to you an everlasting light, and your God your glory," David wrote, "The LORD [YHWH] is my LIGHT" (Psalm 27:1).

Jesus asked, in prayer to the Father, before He went to the cross, that He would share His eternal glory. "O Father, glorify Me together with Yourself, with the glory which I had with You before the world was" (John 17:5). He also spoke of Himself as the coming bridegroom (see Matt. 25:1), which is how *YHWH* is characterized (see Isa. 62:5; Hosea 2:16).

In Revelation 1:17, Jesus says He is the First and Last, which is identical with what *YHWH* says of Himself (see Isa. 44:6). There is no question that He understood Himself to be the Lord (*YHWH*) of the Old Testament. When He was arrested, He used the same name, and this had an electrifying effect on those in the party. "Now when He said to them, 'I am *He*,' they drew back and fell to the ground" (John 18:6).

Notice that "He" is in italics, indicating that the word was added by the translators and is not in the original Greek. However; their attempt to make Jesus' answer more grammatically correct obscures the fact that He was again claiming to be the "I AM" of the Old Testament Scriptures. The apostle Paul affirms that He is the God of the Old Testament to whom the Jews looked as their Rock of strength. "[A]ll our fathers were under the cloud… all ate the same spiritual food, and all drank… of that spiritual Rock that followed them, and that Rock was Christ" (1 Cor. 10:1, 3, 4; see also Deut. 32:4; Ps. 18:2).

Jesus was the One who spoke to Moses and told him to return to Egypt to bring the Israelites to freedom. He was the Lord (*YHWH*) who caused the plagues to fall on Egypt. He was the God who led the Israelites through their wilderness wanderings for forty years. He was the Lawgiver who gave the commandments to Moses and spoke with him on a regular basis. Jesus was the Lord who dealt with Israel throughout their national history.

Yes, astounding as it seems, Jesus Christ is the Lord (*YHWH*) spoken of so often in the Old Testament. He made another statement that aroused the Jews' anger: "I and *My* Father are one" (John 10:30). That is, the Father and Son are both divine. Again, there was no mistaking the intent of what He said, because, "the Jews took up stones again to stone Him" (v. 31). But Jesus countered, "'Many good works I have shown you from My Father. For which of those works do you stone Me?' The Jews answered Him, saying, 'For a good work we do not stone You, but for blasphemy, and because You, being a Man, make Yourself God'" (vs. 32, 33).

The Jews understood perfectly well what Jesus meant. He was telling them plainly of His divinity. He claimed authority to forgive sins. When He healed the paralyzed man, He also said to him, "Son, your sins are forgiven you" (Mark 2:5). The scribes who heard this reasoned among themselves that He was blaspheming, because, as they correctly understood asked, "Who can forgive sins but God alone?" Jesus replied, "'Why do you reason about these things in your hearts? …But that you may know that the Son of Man has power on earth to forgive sins'—He said to the paralytic, 'I say to you, arise, take up your bed, and go to your house'" (vs. 7–11).

Again, the Lord (*YHWH*) is presented in the Old Testament as the One who forgives sins (see Jer. 31:34). Jesus claimed to have the power to raise the dead—a power that God alone possesses.

> For the Father raises the dead and gives life to *them*, even so the Son gives life to whom He will.… Most assuredly, I say to you, the hour is coming, and now is, when the dead will hear the voice of the Son of God; and those who hear will live… all who are in the graves will hear His voice and come forth—those who have done good, to the

resurrection of life, and those who have done evil, to the resurrection of condemnation." (John 5:21, 25, 28, 29)

When Jesus resurrected Lazarus from the dead, He said to his sister Martha, "I am the resurrection and the life" (11:25). Additionally, "The LORD [*YHWH*] kills and makes alive; He brings down to the grave and brings up" (1 Sam. 2:6).

Jesus accepted honor and worship. He declared His divinity in yet another way when He said, "all should honor the Son just as they honor the Father" (John 5:23). He repeatedly told His disciples to believe in Him as they would believe in God (see 14:1). Jesus accepted worship on many occasions without forbidding it. In Matthew 8:2, a leper worshipped Him. A ruler worshipped Him with his petition to raise his daughter from the dead (see 9:18). He stilled the angry waves of the stormy sea, and those in the boat worshipped Him as the Son of God (see 14:32, 33). A Canaanite woman worshipped Jesus (see 15:25).

When Jesus met the women who came to His tomb on resurrection morning, they worshipped Him, and so did His apostles (see 28:9, 17). The demon-possessed man of the Gadarenes worshipped Him (see Mark 5:6). The blind man whom Jesus healed worshipped Him (see John 9:38). The first and second commandments forbid worship of anyone except God alone (see Ex. 20:3–5). Paul and Barnabas were very disturbed when the people tried to worship them after they healed a disabled man in Lystra (see Acts 14:11–15).

In Revelation 22:8–9, when John fell down to worship the angel, the angel refused to accept it. Jesus not only told His followers to believe in Him, but that when we pray to the Father, we are to pray in His name: "And whatever you ask in My name, that I will do, that the Father may be glorified in the Son" (John 14:13). He left no doubt that access comes through Him, telling us that "No one comes to the Father except through Me" (v. 6).

Concerning Jesus, the apostle Paul wrote, "Therefore God has highly exalted Him and given Him the name which is above every name, that at the name of Jesus every knee should bow, of those in heaven, and of those on earth, and of those under the earth, and *that* every tongue should confess that Jesus Christ *is* Lord, to the glory of God the father" (Phil. 2:9–11). Jesus knew He was unique because of His close relationship with the Father, for He was the only One who could reveal Him to humanity. He said, "All things have been delivered to Me by My Father, and no one knows the Son except the Father. Nor does anyone know the Father except the Son, and *the one* to whom the Son wills to reveal *Him*" (Matt. 11:27).

Jesus, by enshrouding His deity with our human nature (though He had no sin), was able to feel our struggles and weaknesses. By giving His life in our place, He is able to redeem us to God the Father. That is the reason the Scripture declares that Jesus is our perfect High Priest, more sympathizing than were the priests of Aaron's line. These priests lived and then died, and they too were sinners who needed a savior. The Bible says that Christ is a high priest forever after the order of Melchizedek.

> For unto which of the angels said he at any time, Thou art my Son, this day have I begotten Thee? And again, I will be to him a Father, and he shall be to me a Son? ... But unto the Son *he saith*, Thy throne, O God, *is* for ever and ever: a sceptre of righteousness *is* the sceptre of Thy kingdom.... And, Thou, Lord, in the beginning hast laid the foundation of the earth; and the heavens are the works of thine hands: They shall perish, but thou remainest; and they all shall wax old as doth a garment; And as a vesture shalt thou fold them up, and they shall be changed: but thou art the same, and thy years shall not fail." (Hebrews 1:5, 8, 10–12, KJV)

This passage ought to make clear to anyone that Jesus Christ is eternal like the Father is. He, by His substitutionary suffering and death, burial, and resurrection, reconciled all those who put their faith in Him, that they may have eternal life. Jesus has called us to take up the cross and follow Him, reminding us that there is no crown without a cross.

The Christians' journey from earth to glory is a walk of faith in Jesus. Paul's Christ-centered message in Ephesians 5 is that we should walk, not as the world walks, but in the light of the grace and mercies of God emanating through our Lord and Savior, as well as pray that by the Holy Spirit's power, we may live as children of light and find out what pleases God, having nothing to do with the unfruitful works of darkness.

As we await the return of our Lord and Savior Jesus Christ, let us endeavor to remain spiritually awake, thereby avoiding the pitfalls that the enemy of our souls places in our pathway. We must be very careful, therefore, how we live, and in a state of readiness, for we know that the day of His coming is nearer than when we first believed. Let us be prayerful and watchful, loving one another as we faithfully wait for that day.

> *As we await the return of our Lord and Savior Jesus Christ, let us endeavor to remain spiritually awake, thereby avoiding the pitfalls that the enemy of our souls places in our pathway.*

CHAPTER 18

Jesus, the Heart of the Gospel

This chapter is based on 1 Corinthians 15. I suggest that this is the most pivotal portion of the epistle because it contains the most indispensable truth of Christianity. If Paul's argument is valid, then Christianity is valid, and this passage opens to us the most elevated and glorious prospect that can be presented to dying mortals. Jesus is the central theme of the Bible. It is His story, from Genesis to Revelation. All of it is about Him, the Lamb of God for sinners slain.

Jesus is the central theme of the Bible. It is His story, from Genesis to Revelation. All of it is about Him, the Lamb of God for sinners slain.

"Moreover, brethren, I declare to you the gospel [good news] which I preached to you, which also you received and in which you stand (1 Cor. 15:1). Everything about the life of Christ is of the utmost importance to believers. The practical consequences of the doctrine of the resurrection of Jesus testified to Saul, who became Paul and a living witness to the living Lord. He met Christ as he was on his way to Damascus to persecute the church, and this became a meeting that he would not soon forget. He would now be asking himself, 'How could I have been so wrong?'

As time would tell, God was about to use this warrior in His service in a very mighty way. Paul would, from this time forward, become a fearless soldier in God's army. He would be known as the apostle to the Gentiles serve Jesus in boldness and forthrightness. He would take the gospel of the kingdom of God to far-flung areas and, by his oratory skills, expound with clarity the doctrines in yet-unentered parts of the Roman Empire and eventually Rome itself, delivering that which he had received (see v. 3).

"[B]y which also you are saved, if you hold fast that word which I preached to you—unless you believed in vain" (v. 2). Salvation comes through faith in Jesus Christ, who shed His blood for the remission of our sins. Those who do not believe cannot be saved (see John 3:3, 16).

"For I delivered unto you first of all that which I also received, how that Christ died for our sins according to the Scriptures: And that He was buried, and that He rose again the third day according to the Scriptures" (1 Cor. 15:3, 4). Christ's substitutionary death, burial, and resurrection were sufficient to pay the penalty for our sins and redeem us to God. He was buried, but raised on the third day, according to the Scriptures. By including both Jesus' death and resurrection as essential elements of the gospel, Paul precluded those who denied the resurrection from claiming salvation in Christ.

"[A]nd that He was seen by Cephas, then by the twelve" (v. 5). This was the same testimony preached by the other disciples. This gospel, which Paul endeavored to pass on down even to our time in history, was also verified by the other apostles, as well as "by over five hundred brethren at once, of whom the greater part remain to the present, but some have fallen asleep" (v. 6).

"After that He was seen by James, then by all the apostles. Then last of all He was seen by me also, as by one born out of due time" (vs. 7, 8). If Christ did not rise from the grave and live forever, then we who believe are still hopelessly dead in our sins.

"For I am the least of the apostles, who am not worthy to be called an apostle, because I persecuted the church of God" (v. 9). Paul never failed to verbalize His regret for having persecuted the church. He was sincere in his sorrow. There are many who sincerely and, in error, mistakenly erred in denying the Lord. Many converts to the early church were formerly among those who refused to accept the message that the Messiah brought to His people. However, after the resurrection, and definitely on the day of Pentecost, there were among those who were present many of the priests and leaders who were convinced when they heard the stirring sermon delivered by Simon Peter. Many of them were converted.

We should never fail to recall that many of those who accepted God's salvation that day were Jews who were among the members of that early church. All the early evangelists who delivered the gospel of Jesus Christ were Jews. We owe them a lot for bringing this message and passing it down to our day. Now it is our turn to use whatever means available to us in passing it on to others. May God grant us the Holy Spirit's power to do so. It is later in earth's history than we may think. Let us, therefore, get busy, and He will supply the resources to do our part.

Paul shared the story of his conversion and the dramatic way in which Jesus Christ met him on the Damascus road as he was hastening to find and persecute those who had come to know of the good news of salvation. Here is something that all must understand: The love of God is immeasurable. "But by the grace of God I am what I am, and His grace toward me was not in vain; but I labored more abundantly than they all, yet not I, but the grace of God *which was* with me. Therefore, whether *it was* I or they, so we preach and so you believed" (vs. 10, 11). The main thing is that we have come to faith in Jesus Christ. Now we are to tell others who also need to know the message of the gospel of God's salvation.

"Now if Christ is preached that He has been raised from the dead, how do some among you say that there is no resurrection of the dead" (v. 12)? People cannot claim to be Christians and deny Jesus' resurrection from the dead. They also need to hear the gospel. Start at the beginning and tell the story of God's expansive love and grace. Oh yes, tell it to them; tell them repeatedly salvation's story, over and over, until none can dare say, "Nobody has ever told me that story before." Everyone needs to hear of God's great love.

"But if there is no resurrection of the dead, then Christ is not risen" (v. 13). Just keep telling the story in all its simplicity, far and wide. Even those who now may not choose to believe the message still need to hear it. They, in time, will either come to understand and believe or refuse to accept the message of the gospel of God's salvation through Jesus Christ.

Either way, they will never be able to say they have never been told. How one responds is up to that person.

"And if Christ is not risen, then our preaching *is* empty and your faith *is* also empty" (v. 14). Bodily resurrection was essential to the gospel. Without Christ's resurrection, the gospel would be false and meaningless.

"Yes, and we are found false witnesses of God, because we have testified of God that He raised up Christ, whom He did not raise up—if in fact the dead do not rise. For if *the* dead do not rise, then Christ is not risen" (vs. 15, 16). At the time in history when the Savior came to earth to show humanity who God is really like, of those who refused to believe, after the resurrection, a large number changed their minds when they realized that the disciples were now far more resolute after the resurrection than they were before. They came to understand that it was the resurrection that made the difference.

Before, they were doubtful and skeptical, but afterward, they were like steel—resolute and firm in their convictions. They could not be shaken. When the Master was teaching them, they trusted Him and wanted to believe, but what they were hearing sounded strange in their ears. They did not understand.

However, when they remembered the things that He taught them, began to connect the dots, and became filled with the Holy Spirit at Pentecost, their eyes and ears were opened, and everything suddenly clicked. Nothing could stop them now as they received power from on high. They were convinced, and their minds were enlightened. There was nothing on this earth that could stifle their enthusiasm.

> And if Christ is not risen, your faith *is* futile; you are still in your sins! Then also those who have fallen asleep in Christ have perished. If in this life only we have hope in Christ, we are of all men most pitiable. But now Christ is risen from the dead, *and* has become the firstfruits of those who have fallen asleep. For since by man *came* death, by Man also *came* the resurrection from the dead.

> For as in Adam all die, even so in Christ all shall be made alive. But each one in his own order: Christ the firstfruits, afterward those *who are* Christ's at His coming. Then *comes* the end, when He delivers the kingdom to God the Father, when He puts an end to all rule and all authority and power. For He must reign till He has put all enemies under His feet. The last enemy *that* will be destroyed *is* death. For "He has put all things under His feet." But when He says "all things are put under *Him*," *it is* evident that He who put all things under Him is excepted. Now when all things are made subject to Him, then the Son Himself will also be subject to Him who put all things under Him, that God may be all in all. Otherwise, what will they do who are baptized for the dead, if the dead do not rise at all? Why then are they baptized for the dead? And why do we stand in jeopardy every hour? I affirm, by the boasting in you which I have in Christ Jesus our Lord, I die daily. If, in the manner of men, I have fought with beasts at Ephesus, what advantage *is it* to me? If *the* dead do not rise, "Let us eat and drink, for tomorrow we die!" Do not be deceived: "Evil company corrupts good habits." (1 Corinthians 15:17–33)

How very true this closing statement is (of course, the whole passage is inspired). For this very reason, believers today need to be alert to the snares of the devil as he seeks opportunities to snatch them away. Let us be prepared for Satan's wiles, lest we are deceived at the last hour. Remember Jesus' words: "[H]old fast… till I come" (Rev. 2:25). We need to prevent becoming ensnared by the culture and be patiently watchful for the appearing of our Lord and Savior Jesus Christ.

The term "evil company" alludes to a close companionship or association. We are less horrified by vice when we're more familiar with it and therefore tend to lose our spirituality.

> Since all are greatly influenced by those with whom they associate… Paul exhorted the believers to beware of the smooth and plausible arguments of the false teachers who denied the resurrection of the dead. The company of such individuals is to be avoided. Association with those who hold erroneous opinions, or whose lives are impure, has a tendency to corrupt the faith and morals of believers. By daily association with those who did not believe in the resurrection of the dead, and by frequent conversation on that topic, the believers would be likely to lose their clear, positive understanding of the truth. Familiarity with error tends to remove objection to it and to lessen caution against it. For this reason God has always counseled His people to separate themselves from close association with unbelievers. (White, *The SDA Bible Commentary*, vol 6, pp. 808, 809)

"Awake to righteousness, and do not sin; for some do not have the knowledge of God. I speak *this* to your shame. But someone will say, 'How are the dead raised up? And with what body do they come'" (1 Cor. 15:34, 35)? The natural mind raises objections to the idea of a resurrection of the dead.

"Foolish one, what you sow is not made alive unless it dies" (v. 36). Here we have a reference to agriculture, which Jesus so frequently used for clarity.

"And what you sow, you do not sow that body that shall be, but mere grain—perhaps wheat or some other *grain*. But God gives it a body as He pleases, and to each seed its own body" (vs. 37, 38).

> There is nothing in the kernel itself that, unaided, causes it to spring into life… Likewise there is nothing in the disintegrating body of the dead that, of itself, leads to the resurrection. But God has arranged that there should be a resurrection, and it is by His power alone that the miracle

takes place. In the resurrection each one will have a body that is appropriate for him. The righteous will have glorified bodies, and the wicked will rise with bodies bearing the marks of their lost state. (White, *The SDA Bible Commentary*, vol 6, pp. 809, 810)

All flesh *is* not the same flesh, but *there is* one *kind of* flesh of men, another flesh of animals, another of fish, *and* another of birds. *There are* also celestial bodies and terrestrial bodies; but the glory of the celestial *is* one, and the *glory* of the terrestrial *is* another. *There is* one glory of the sun, another glory of the moon, and another glory of the stars; for *one* star differs from *another* star in glory. So also *is* the resurrection of the dead. *The body* is sown in corruption, it is raised in incorruption. (1 Corinthians 15:39–42)

Paul speaks of the bodies of the redeemed as a seed sown in the ground, which will produce a harvest for God's kingdom. The graveyard is sometimes appropriately called "God's acre." The dissolution that quietly goes on there, out of sight, is preliminary to the glorious resurrection when the winter of this world's history is past and the eternal spring dawns with the coming of our Lord and Savior Jesus Christ (see 1 Cor. 15:52; 1 Thess. 4:16). Paul affirms that the resurrection of the righteous dead, with glorified bodies, will take place. This is one of the most encouraging truths that can be presented to those who, in this life, are wasting away with disease and looking forward with dread to the grave.

"It is sown in dishonor, it is raised in glory. It is sown in weakness, it is raised in power" (1 Cor. 15:43). "Dignity, beauty, honor, and perfection will characterize the resurrected saints, whose bodies have been made like unto that of Christ" (White 1956, p. 810).

"It is sown a natural body, it is raised a spiritual body. There is a natural body, and there is a spiritual body. And so it is written, 'The first man Adam became a living being.' The last Adam *became* a life-giving spirit" (1 Cor. 15:44, 45). "Adam became a 'living soul,' but Christ is the life-giver. Jesus said that He had power to raise the dead... He exercised this power in relation to this temporal, earthly life by raising certain ones from the dead… These demonstrations of His power to give life may be accepted as evidence of His power to raise the dead at His second advent" (White 1956, p. 811).

"However, the spiritual is not first, but the natural, and afterward the spiritual. The first man *was* of the earth, *made* of dust; the second Man *is* the Lord from heaven" (1 Cor. 15:46, 47). Paul here is stating that mankind's present body, made of flesh and blood, is unfit for entrance into God's heavenly abode. Our new bodies will be fashioned like the glorious, resurrected body of Jesus Christ (see Phil. 3:21).

It is the opinion of some interpreters that it may be deduced that resurrected bodies will not have flesh and blood. "As *is* the earthy, such *are* they also that are earthy: and as *is* the heavenly, such *are* they also that are heavenly. And as we have borne the image of the earthly, we shall also bear the image of the heavenly. Now this I say, brethren, that flesh and blood cannot inherit the kingdom of God; neither doth corruption inherit incorruption" (1 Cor. 15:48–50, KJV). The reason for this assumption seems to be found in the second part of the statement, namely—the impossibility of corruption inheriting incorruption.

"Behold, I shew you a mystery; We shall not all sleep, but we shall all be changed, In a moment, in the twinkling of an eye, at the last trump: for the trumpet shall sound, and the dead shall be raised incorruptible, and we shall be changed" (vs. 51, 52, KJV). This phrase points to the rapidity with which the change will occur, the time for which being when Jesus comes the second time to take His saints to heaven. It is at that time that those who have died in Christ will be called from their sleep in the earth to meet Him. Then the Christians who are alive will unite with those who have been asleep and were awakened by the call of God.

"The time when this glorious transformation… will be at the second coming of Christ, for it is then that the 'trump of God' will sound, and faithful believers who have died will be raised in bodies that are entirely free from all effects of sin" (White 1956, p. 812).

"For this corruptible must put on incorruption, and this mortal *must* put on immortality" (1 Cor. 15:53). The earthly bodies will be transformed into resurrected bodies, no longer subject to sickness and corruption. They will meet the Lord in the air and together have the wonderful experience of being taken to heaven. There will then be no more pain or malady; no inflammatory process caused by disease; for no sin or anything that mars or defiles will be allowed to enter there (see Nah. 1:9; Rev. 21:4).

"So when this corruptible has put on incorruption, and this mortal has put on immortality, then shall be brought to pass the saying that is written, 'Death is swallowed up in victory" (1 Cor. 15:54). "When, at Christ's coming, the amazing transformation from mortal to immortal has taken place, both of the righteous dead and the righteous living, then man's great enemy will no longer trouble the redeemed.... As they see that Christ has come and conferred on them the gift of immortality, their first sensation will be one of great rejoicing that never again will they succumb to the power of death" (White 1956, p. 813).

"O death, where *is* thy sting? O grave, where *is* thy victory" (1 Cor. 15:55, KJV)? In this glad, victorious cry both death and the grave are here personified and addressed (White 1956, p. 813). Since the fall of Adam, sin has caused the sting of death to hold sway over God's creation, but will do so no more.

"The sting of death is sin; and the strength of sin is the law. But thanks be to God, who gives the victory through our Lord Jesus Christ" (1 Cor. 15:56, 57). "This verse presents the theme" of all Scripture, "to show that the restoration of man to favor with God and to his original condition of perfection and freedom from all the effects of sin, is brought about by the mighty power of God working through our Lord Jesus Christ" (White 1956, p. 813).

"Therefore, my beloved brethren, be ye steadfast, unmovable, always abounding in the work of the Lord, forasmuch as ye know that your labour is not in vain in the Lord" (1 Cor. 15:58). "In view of the glorious truth that has been revealed concerning the resurrection, believers are exhorted to resist every effort that may be made by the agents of Satan to undermine their faith in Christ.... Believers are urged to remain firm in their faith," immovable and uncompromising. "No person or thing is to be permitted to shake the believer from the foundation of his faith and hope" (White

1956, p. 813). The return of Jesus should be the theme of every Christian's life. Therefore, may we often utter this prayer: "Maranatha—Come Lord Jesus! Amen!

Please listen to what I'm about to say: Everything that Jesus said to those humble fishermen has come to pass, and all the prophecies He taught in Matthew 24 and 25 are definitely being fulfilled. The messages that God gave the prophet Daniel are rapidly unfolding, and Jesus Christ is coming soon. Are you ready? The people in Noah's day refused to believe; then God's hands closed the door of the ark, and it was too late. Their probation had come and passed by them.

Lot daughters and their husbands laughed at him when he told them the city would be destroyed. His wife was told not to look back, but she had become too much a part of Sodom, so she looked back and became a pillar of salt. It was too late. Jesus is coming soon—sooner than we may believe. There is nothing here on earth that is more valuable than our connection to the God of heaven and earth. Jesus shed His blood on Calvary's cross that we might have eternal life. He invites us to "Come unto Me, all *you* who labor and are heavy laden, and I will give you rest. Take My yoke upon you and learn of Me… for My… burden is light" (Matt. 11:28–30).

> The coming King is at the door,
> Who once the cross for sinners bore,
> But now the righteous ones alone,
> He comes to gather home.
>
> The signs that show His coming near
> Are fast fulfilling year by year,
> And soon we'll hail the glorious dawn,
> Of heav'n's eternal morn.
>
> At the door, at the door,
> At the door, yes, even at the door;
> He is coming, He is coming,
> He is even at the door. (by F.E. Belden, 1886)

CHAPTER 19

What Will Heaven Be Like?

And he showed me a pure river of water of life, clear as crystal, proceeding from the throne of God and of the Lamb. In the middle of its street, and on either side of the river, *was* a tree of life, which bore twelve fruits, each *tree* yielding its fruit every month. The leaves of the tree *were* for the healing of the nations. (Revelation 22:1, 2)

Now I saw a new heaven and a new earth, for the first heaven and the first earth had passed away. Also there was no more sea. Then I, John, saw the holy city, New Jerusalem, coming down out of heaven from God, prepared as a bride adorned for her husband. And I heard a loud voice from heaven saying, "Behold, the tabernacle of God *is* with men, and He will dwell with them, and they shall be His people. God Himself will be with them *and be* their God. And God will wipe away every tear from their eyes; there shall be no more death, nor sorrow, nor crying. There shall be no more pain, for the former things have passed away." (Revelation 21:1–4)

The angel who was still with John had been his guide since the beginning of this vision. In the center of the New Jerusalem was the river of the water of life that gushed from the throne of God. Ezekiel prophesied that a river flowing from the temple of a restored, earthly Jerusalem, down to the Dead Sea, would bring abundant life to that most barren spot in the world (see 47:1). A river nourished the Garden of Eden (see Gen. 2:10). Now a life-giving river nourishes New Jerusalem.

The essential meaning of this river finds fulfillment in Jesus' declaration to the woman at the well of Sychar: "[W]hoever drinks of the water that I shall give him will never thirst. But the water that I shall give him will become in him a fountain of water springing up into everlasting life" (John 4:14). John portrays that eternal life is entirely due to God's gracious gift. The river flowing from His throne depicts this reality.

As we go through this brief study, we will see that there is more to tell about the city that Jesus has gone to prepare than time would allow us here. You may have noticed that I have not yet mentioned the streets paved with gold as clear as glass or the walls of jasper and gates of pearls. All those things will be nice to see, but my friends, I must humbly submit that nothing can compare to the fact that God the Father, Jesus Christ, and the Holy Spirit will be there. Their presence is what will make heaven worth it all for me. We will be able to see the face of God, as well as Jesus' nail-scarred hands and feet and thorn-scarred brow.

You may have noticed that I have not yet mentioned the streets paved with gold as clear as glass or the walls of jasper and gates of pearls. All those things will be nice to see, but my friends, I must humbly submit that nothing can compare to the fact that God the Father, Jesus Christ, and the Holy Spirit will be there.

There are many different interpretations regarding the exact architecture of this city. It may be unclear for one very good reason: when Jesus was on earth, He told His disciples that His father has many abiding places (or mansions or rooms). Many Bible interpreters ask, "Besides the celestial grandeur that marks the uniqueness of the environment, what makes heaven an entirely different place?"

One might ponder the necessity of this question had it not been for the fact that severe changes in the culture in these closing days of time are taking place all over the world. Is it the great celestial structures of dreamlike grandeur? Is it the streets paved with gold? Is it the uniqueness of the main street with the tree of life—one single plant with its different fruit each month? Or should we take "tree" to be a collection of individual plants standing on each side of the river of life?

Since there seems to be such a variation of possibilities, perhaps we ought to wait until we get there and not speculate. As Christ Himself said, "No one has ascended to heaven but He who came down from heaven" (John 3:13). However, we ought to take a closer look at the tree of life, since it is the only vegetation mentioned here as part of the eternal state and a feature that reminds us of the Garden of Eden.

In Revelation 2:7, Jesus pledged, "To him who overcomes I will give to eat from the tree of life, which is in the midst of the Paradise of God." In this we find the promise of the complete removal of the curse. After the fall, God lovingly declared that mankind must not be allowed to reach out the hand, take from the tree of life, eat, and live forever (see Gen. 3:22). However, now that the curse is gone, the overcomers may eat. Just as drinking the water symbolizes everlasting life, so eating the fruit symbolizes all the divine blessings of the eternal state.

In Ezekiel's vision, the life-giving river had an amazing and unimaginable impact on various fruit trees. "Along the bank of the river, on this side and that, will grow all *kinds of* trees used for food; their leaves will not wither, and their fruit will not fail. They will bear fruit every month, because their water flows from the sanctuary. Their fruit will be for food, and their leaves for medicine" (47:12).

The trees and their fruit-bearing schedule symbolize God's unceasing, limitless blessings. Some Bible interpreters point out that since there is no need for the moon to give light, there may also be an absence of the months since the moon currently marks the passage of time. There will be no need to mark the passage of time, for why be concerned with the passage of eternity? Our great and wonderful God has many surprises in store for us, for He inspired the apostle to write, "Eye has not seen, nor ear heard, nor have entered into the heart of man The things which God has prepared for those who love Him" (1 Cor. 2:9).

However grand and majestic all these structures will be in the city of God, I venture to suggest that heaven will be distinguished by the presence of the eternal Godhead, for the Father, Son, and Holy Spirit will be there. All the grandeur, luster, and architectural delights that will surpass all the magnificent luminescence that awaits us would be incomplete without the presence of the Ancient of Days, the Lamb slain from before the foundation of the world, and the Comforter.

Their presence will be the crowning joy and wonder that top the exquisite delight that will make heaven a place of paradise.

> Once Heaven seemed a far-off place,
> Till Jesus showed His smiling face;
> Now, it's begun within my soul,
> 'Twill last while endless ages roll.
>
> O hallelujah yes, 'tis Heav'n,
> Tis Heav'n to know my sins forgiv'n;
> On land or sea, no matter where?
> Where Jesus is, 'tis heaven there. (by Charles F. Butler)

Perhaps I should not speculate, but I can imagine, can't I? I believe the tree of life, the fruit of which the redeemed will eat in heaven, is the same tree that was in the midst of the Garden of Eden, from which our first parents were prevented from eating, lest their misery, caused by sin, would have lasted eternally. God sent the flaming sword to guard the tree for the protection of Adam and Eve and their posterity.

This is evidence of God's everlasting love. He sent His only begotten Son to die for us and redeem us all from the curse. Oh, what a God, oh;

what a Savior! What will heaven be like? Sometimes I wonder as, with great expectancy, I look for the return of Jesus, our Redeemer, King of kings, and Lord of lords. As I view the deteriorating conditions in our world, I look towards the eastern skies and pray, "Come, Lord Jesus; come soon."

The leaves of the tree of life are for the healing of the nations. In heaven, there will be no sickness, pain, death, sorrow, or sin, for Jesus our Savior and God Himself will be there. There will be no sun, for Jesus, the Son of righteousness, will be the light source. Ask any number of people what will heaven be like, and you are likely to get a similar number of descriptions. There will be no more senseless murders; no more killing of unwanted babies; no more brutality; no harsh treatment of those who are poor, and helpless; no more senseless greed; No more potbelly children dying of hunger, even when there is far more food wasted in the world than there are those in need.

We will see the face of the One whom we adore. Revelation 4 tells us that John saw the presence of God in the throne room of the universe. He saw all His creatures prostrating themselves and worshipping Him day and night. There were four living creatures around the throne who worshipped, saying, "Holy, Holy, Holy." There were twenty-four elders on thrones, with crowns on their heads, and when the four living creatures bowed down to worship God, the twenty-four elders all fell and worshipped Him also, and all creation joined in united worship day and night, for He is worthy of all glory, honor, and praise.

Here in this earthly life, God's servants only halfheartedly serve Him in worship with incomplete obedience. In heaven, the first blessing will be faultless, active adoration and praise. The second blessing will be His immediate presence. God's name will be on the foreheads of His people. To bear His name will be counted a privilege and blessing. The concluding blessing will be that those in heaven will reign with God and Christ forever and ever. Jesus says, "He who has an ear, let him hear what the Spirit says to the churches:" (Rev. 2:29).

The Scriptures present us with a description of heaven. John describes what he saw when he was invited in a vision to visit God's throne room. I recommend you read Revelation 4 before continuing. The apostle is in awe as his attention is now directed to a symbolic vision of the throne of God. He describes it as made of jasper and Sardius stones, with a rainbow-like emerald encircling it. This throne room is described as the holiest place in the entire universe and, particularly, the heavenly sanctuary, where God the Father and Christ our Great High Priest dwell. John is reverently reticent in avoiding any ascription of human attributes to God.

We are called upon to remember that Moses asked to see the face of God on the mountain and was told, "no man shall see Me, and live" (Ex. 33:20). Before the throne was a sea of glass like crystal. In the midst of and around the throne were the four living creatures, full of eyes in front and back. Elsewhere, these four living creatures are described as representing all of God's creation, including mankind.

Thus, when we come to worship God, we essentially and spiritually do so in a congregational context. Revelation 21 gives us a broad glimpse of the structural layout of the celestial abode of the paradise of God and Jesus Christ with all the redeemed after sin has been eliminated. This very earth will be cleansed and purified after the millennium has passed and become the capital of the entire universe.

Thus, when we come to worship God, we essentially and spiritually do so in a congregational context.

This very earth on which we now dwell will be cleansed of all evil. The struggle between good and evil, right and wrong, God and Satan, will finally be over. The hearts and minds of those who find refuge will in this life have been cleansed and purified of all rebellion against God. Sin and Satan will be no more; sickness and death will not even be a memory, for the Bible says all things will be made new. There will be no more wars. Peace will forever reign.

The Bible tells us that God will make all things new and wipe away all tears from our eyes. The prophet Nahum wrote, "Behold, on the mountains

The feet of him who brings good tidings, Who proclaims peace! O Judah, keep your appointed feasts, Perform your vows. For the wicked one shall no more pass through you; He is utterly cut off" (1:15). The long controversy between Christ and Satan will be over. The Father has promised that peace will reign eternally, for His Son has conquered the grave.

The Lord will be with the redeemed and be their God. Jesus shall reign on the earth forever. For anyone who may be thinking that all this is only a dream, go to your Bibles, look at the prophecies, and read of their fulfillments. God has kept every promise He has ever made. He is a promise-keeping God. The Lamb slain from before the foundation of the world will reign on the earth.

> Blessed *are* those who do His commandments, that they may have the right to the tree of life, and may enter through the gates into the city.... "I, Jesus, have sent My angel to testify to you these things in the churches. I am the Root and the Offspring of David, the Bright and Morning Star.... Surely I am coming quickly." Amen. Even so, come, Lord Jesus! The grace of our Lord Jesus Christ *be* with you all. Amen. (Revelation 22:14, 16, 20, 21)

Bibliography

Branson, W.H. *Drama of the Ages.* Maranatha Media, 2002.

Collins Dictionary.

Geisler, Norman L. *Christian Apologetics.* Grand Rapids, MI: Baker Book House.

Lewis, C.S. *Mere Christianity.* 1952.

Maxwell, C. Mervyn, *God Cares*, *Vol. 1.* Nampa, ID: Pacific Press Publishing Association, 1981.

McGee, J. Vernon. *Thru the Bible*, *Vol. 4.* Nashville: Thomas Nelson Publishers, 1983.

White, Ellen G. *The Desire of Ages.* Mountain View, CA: Pacific Press Publishing Association, 1898.

White, Ellen G. *Lift Him Up.* Hagerstown, MD: Review and Herald Publishing Association, 1988.

White, Ellen G. *Patriarchs and Prophets.* Washington, DC: Review and Herald Publishing Association, 1890.

White, Ellen G. *The SDA Bible Commentary. Vol. 5.* Washington, DC: Review and Herald Publishing Association, 1956.

White, Ellen G. *The SDA Bible Commentary. Vol. 6.* Washington, DC: Review and Herald Publishing Association, 1956.

White, Ellen G. *The SDA Bible Commentary. Vol. 7.* Washington, DC: Review and Herald Publishing Association, 1957.

White, Ellen G. *That I May Know Him.* Washington, DC: Review and Herald Publishing Association, 1964.

We invite you to view the complete
selection of titles we publish at:
www.TEACHServices.com

We encourage you to write us
with your thoughts about this,
or any other book we publish at:
info@TEACHServices.com

TEACH Services' titles may be purchased in
bulk quantities for educational, fund-raising,
business, or promotional use.
bulksales@TEACHServices.com

Finally, if you are interested in seeing
your own book in print, please contact us at:
publishing@TEACHServices.com
We are happy to review your manuscript at no charge.

www.ingramcontent.com/pod-product-compliance
Lightning Source LLC
Chambersburg PA
CBHW070554160426
43199CB00014B/2496